SOURS

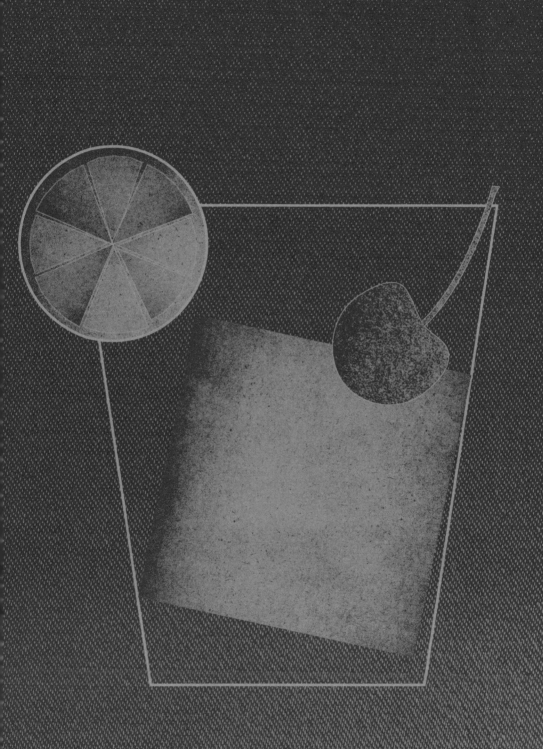

SOURS

A HISTORY OF THE WORLD'S
MOST STORIED COCKTAIL STYLE

Philip Greene

**UNION
SQUARE
& CO.**

NEW YORK

CONTENTS

INTRODUCTION

THE TERM "SOUR COCKTAIL" might not mean anything to you—and might not even sound too terribly appealing. But there you'd be mistaken, for the category of drinks known as "sours" contains some of the most historic, iconic, and delicious cocktails ever known. The magical trinity of sweet, sour, and strong is the basic platform of legendary drinks like the Daiquiri, the Sidecar, the Margarita, the Jack Rose, the Whiskey Sour, the Pisco Sour, the Bee's Knees, the Aviation, and that modern pop culture phenom known as the Cosmopolitan, among too many others to name. In David Embury's epic 1948 cocktail book, *The Fine Art of Mixing Drinks*, he gives us his version of the Mount Rushmore of drinks, formed by "six basic cocktails": the Martini, the Manhattan, the

Old-Fashioned, the Daiquiri, the Sidecar, and the Jack Rose. Notice anything about that esteemed list? *Half of them are sours.*

Citrus fruits, mainly lemon and lime, have been found in drinks going back to the sixteenth century (such as, for example, a key ingredient in punch), and beginning in 1740, the British Royal Navy prescribed a daily ration of rum to be dispensed to crew members along with sugar and lemon or lime juice. This became known as "grog," and the better members of the crew would "receive extra lime juice and sugar that it be made more palatable to them." See the Navy Grog (page 162) for more background on this classic.

Folklore tells of similar drinks. There's the tale of "El Draque," a likely apocryphal story about a sixteenth-century English privateer, Sir Francis Drake. Or was it Captain Richard Drake? Accounts differ. (Did I mention it was probably apocryphal?) In any case, Drake and his crewmen, after failing to capture Havana, sought comfort in a drink composed of aguardiente (unaged rum), lime juice, sugar, and mint, which many sources will want you to believe was the prototype of the Mojito. Then, as long as we're in Cuba, we have the story of Canchánchara, a drink made from light rum, lime juice, and honey. By some accounts, it was the source of nutrition for the early Cuban patriots during their never-ending struggle against the Spanish for independence. So many of these stories are just that—stories—but they are entertaining all the same.

One of the earliest known single-sized cocktails containing citrus is believed (by some) to be the Brandy Crusta (brandy, orange curaçao, lemon juice, bitters), invented in the 1850s by legendary New Orleans bartender Joseph Santini. The earliest-known use of the term "Sour" was seen as a category of drink in an 1856 cocktail menu from Mart Ackermann's Saloon in Toronto, Canada. Bartenders of the nineteenth century—and all the way up to Prohibition, which lasted between 1920 and 1933—became adept at mastering the trinity of spirit, citrus, and sweetener, combining them to create a wide range of drinks, all offshoots on this three-legged barstool, so to speak.

From this classic platform has evolved a wide range of innovative drinks, with the addition of soda water and other fizzy components (including

Champagne), such as the Collins, Mojito, and French 75; and exotic syrups and liqueurs, notably tiki drinks (such as the Mai Tai, Zombie, and Scorpion), frozen drinks (the Daiquiri, Margarita, and others), and even "shot" type drinks, such as the Kamikaze. They're all sours, with the three-part formula of strong, sweet, and sour as a foundation.

So many of these drinks have rich backstories to them. The Daiquiri was a favorite of playwright Tennessee Williams, writer Ernest Hemingway, and President John F. Kennedy (and First Lady Jackie!), and was first featured in F. Scott Fitzgerald's classic 1920 novel *This Side of Paradise*. The Whiskey Sour was the go-to drink during a classic 1925 road trip from Lyon to Paris by none other than Fitzgerald and Hemingway. The tropical decadence of the Margarita helped launch the career of celebrated singer-songwriter Jimmy Buffett, and has sent legions of fans to yearn for some booze in the blender (while searching for that lost shaker of salt). During World War I, one classic Sour had to temporarily change its name to the Royal Smile because a notorious mobster, Jacob "Bald Jack" Rosenzweig, also went by the nickname "Jack Rose." One cannot fully enjoy Raymond Chandler's *The Long Goodbye* or Hemingway's "The Short Happy Life of Francis Macomber" without sipping on a classic Gimlet. And did Hemingway really drink seventeen double frozen Daiquiris at El Floridita in Havana one day in the early 1940s?

Yet what many people (even drinkers) don't understand is that *these drinks are all pretty much built the same way*. I'll never forget a seminar I attended at the Tales of the Cocktail festival in New Orleans, way back in 2004, when my friend (and bartending legend) Audrey Saunders stood before a whiteboard and (without knowing it, thank you, Audrey) gave me the idea for this book. She detailed how versatile the Sour platform was: start with this drink, swap this for that, or add this and this, and you've got this. Swap out the rum and sugar from a Daiquiri and put in applejack and grenadine and it's now a Jack Rose. Change a Whiskey Sour by using honey syrup instead of simple syrup, and now it's a Gold Rush. Then swap the whiskey for gin to make a Bee's Knees. "Extend" that basic Gin Sour with soda water and serve it in a tall glass, on the rocks, and now it's a Tom Collins. Add a splash of cranberry juice to a basic Vodka Sour and what do you get? A Cosmo. Similar to that Tom Collins, add soda water and mint to the classic Daiquiri, and serve it in a tall glass filled with ice and you've made a Mojito. My mind was pretty much blown.

So this book will tell you not only the history and folklore of these classic drinks, but how to make them at home, *and* how to create your own delicious spinoffs from this immortal three-part platform. After all, it's about variation. World-renowned bartender, author, and my friend Jim Meehan (former part-owner of PDT, as in "Please Don't Tell," the groundbreaking East Village speakeasy located, then as now, via a secret door within a phone booth found within a hot dog shop), said it best. In *The Oxford Companion to Spirits and Cocktails* (2021), in the entry titled "Cocktail Variation," he described it as follows:

> Variation can be premeditated, based on a mixological understanding of how the ingredients can be altered without changing the fundamental identity of the recipe, or it can be result from necessity (the lemons didn't come that day) or error, resulting in a variety of outcomes, ranging from an unhappy patron to a new recipe or accepted variation upon the original.
>
> . . . This kind of ingredient switching is known among bartenders as the "Mr. Potato head" method of creating new recipes, after the popular toy, which gives one a selection of facial features that may be substituted for one another.

But the concept of variation is not new. In the late 1940s, David Embury included in his *The Fine Art of Mixing Drinks* a whole chapter called "Roll Your Own." Therein, he encouraged readers to not just *make* cocktails, but to *invent* their own cocktails. "Yet you yourself—anyone—can invent cocktails, good cocktails, palatable cocktails, delicious cocktails, by the dozen—nay, by the hundred. You need no recipe book. All you need is an understanding of a few fundamental principles and a reasonable discriminating taste." (Ironic, isn't it, that within my recipe book I'm telling you about another author's recipe book that tells you that "you need no recipe book"?)

Anyway, Embury's book lays out the various types of cocktail "platforms," beginning with the basic premise that "the essential ingredients of a cocktail are (a) the base and (b) the modifier." With respect to the Sour, Embury explained that "the Sour type is so named not because it tastes sour but because it is patterned after the various Sours, i.e., it consists of lemon or lime juice, sugar or some other sweetening, and a spiritous liquor. If you examine practically any book of cocktail recipes you will find that a very large percentage of the recipes are of this type. This is because the citrus juices blend well with all kinds of spiritous liquors and all kinds of cordials and fruit juices." He further encouraged readers to "roll their own" new cocktails, by taking an existing recipe and swapping out the spirit and/or the sweetener and/or the citrus juice. That's essentially what this book intends to do as well. What's the old expression? "Everything old is new again."

I often hear that mixology is much like cooking: You begin with basic concepts, and you build out from there through trial and error. In the case of drink creation, you start with the Daiquiri, let's say, and you add additional flavorings, such as other juices and/or liqueurs, much the same way that tiki pioneers Donn "Don the Beachcomber" Beach and Victor "Trader Vic" Bergeron did when they created their masterpieces such as the Zombie (page 244), Navy Grog (page 162), Fog Cutter (page 90), Three Dots and a Dash (page 213), and Mai Tai (page 138).

On the culinary side, consider the French school of cooking, and its reliance on the "Mother Sauces"—béchamel, velouté, espagnole, hollandaise, and tomat—which serve as the starting point in so many classic French dishes. Created in in the nineteenth century by French chef Auguste Escoffier, these sauces were found in his seminal work, *Le Guide Culinaire* (1903). Without going too far down this rabbit hole, you can start with béchamel (a milk-based sauce, thickened with a white roux and seasoned with onion, nutmeg, and/or thyme), and from that Mother Sauce make crème, Mornay, soubise, ecossaise, and nantua sauces. Similarly, from espagnole (a brown sauce made from a brown roux and brown stock, such as veal or beef, along with tomato sauce or paste), you can make demi-glace, poivrade, grand veneur, and bigarade sauces.

But, hey, I'd love to talk French cooking all day, but I've got a cocktail book to write! Within the pages of this book, I'll endeavor to present the idea that the Sour cocktail, which of course could be considered a "Daughter Drink" of the Mother of All Drinks (namely punch), herself grew up to become the mother of so many categories of drinks.

Truth be told, I struggled for a while with the organization of this book. Should I start with just the three-ingredient drinks, then move to the four-ingredient ones, then drinks with five ingredients, and so on, continuing to press the point of just how versatile the underlying three-part platform is? But then I realized, no one ever came home from work and said, "Hey, honey, I think we should try some *five-part* drinks this weekend—you know, to *keep things spicy*." Instead, the book is organized alphabetically, with the occasional sidebar or subchapter where I branch out to talk about a particular subfamily of drinks, such as Fizzes, Twenty-First-Century Smashes, Constante Ribalaigua's assortment of Daiquiris at Havana's famed bar El Floridita, the Collins family, and so on.

In assembling my collection of drinks, I soon realized there are too many to include—this book could easily be a thousand pages or more. After all, not only are there untold numbers of great drinks based on the Sour platform but many, many more are being invented (and are yet to be invented) by both professional and home bartenders, including you! And so along with a list of the essential Sours and related cocktails, I included brief mentions of spin-offs of the underlying drink, which I call "Variations." By offering these variations, I was able to shoehorn in many more drinks for you to discover and enjoy.

Mind you, my "here's another great drink, now go look up the recipe" plan does not come without some amount of trepidation, as there are more than a few websites out there that cannot be trusted to give good information on drink recipes. (Yes, you heard it here first: You shouldn't believe everything you read on the interwebs.) So, I hereby offer to you a (partial) list of reputable websites where you're certain to find reliable info: BonAppetit.com, Boothby.com.au, ClassBarMag.com, CraftandCocktails.co, DiffordsGuide.com, Flaviar.com, Ginhound.com, Imbibe.com, KindredCocktails.com, Liquor.com, PunchDrink.com, Saveur.com,

SpruceEats.com, StirAndStrain.com, RobertSimonson.substack.com, and Vinepair.com. There are more, but these I've found to be trustworthy. (One way to discern how credible a site is: Do they use photos that look nothing like the drink the recipe is supposed to represent? "Say, I've seen that lime-green Mojito-looking-thing before . . .")

I've also tried to offer a wide range of great drinks, with the majority being classics (such as the Daiquiri, Margarita, Bee's Knees, Gin Fizz, and Tom Collins), modern classics (such as the Paper Plane, Penicillin, Bramble, and Gold Rush), and excellent drinks created by friends of mine in the industry or drinks I've discovered in my travels.

Further, while this book focuses on the traditional uses of citrus juice, please be mindful of more creative methods and practices of using the components of citrus fruit, namely the peel (see oleosaccharum, page 21, and oleo citrate and Super Juice, page 12), as well as the acid found in the actual juice. For example, there's a commercial offering from Belgium known as Sūpāsawā that's billed as an alternative to citrus juice. It's a distilled water–based product containing five different types of acid—citric, malic, tartaric, succinic, and phosphoric—along with a little sugar and salt, and is intended to mimic the sourness, flavor, and "zing" of citrus juice. Lastly, if you want to do a deeper dive into the study of the use of acids in cocktails, check out the teachings of Dave Arnold, author of *Liquid Intelligence: The Art and Science of the Perfect Cocktail.*

Back to the drinks! With just a couple of exceptions, I tried to select cocktails that are easy(ish) for the home bartender to make, and that won't break the bank or cause you to spend hours making some sort of honey/thyme/green tea tincture. As an amateur bartender myself, I try to keep things simple, by mastering basic formulas in inventing new drinks and leaving the "molecular mixology" and the really sophisticated stuff to the pros, just as I'd do with cooking. In writing this book, I tried to stick to the guidance of drinks writer Kingsley Amis, who offered these pearls of wisdom in his 2008 book *Everyday Drinking*: "More practically, you will waste a lot of time—unless of course, you were simply using your drinks manual as dipsography, the alcohol equivalent of pornography—reading about concoctions to call for stuff you simply have not got (on) hand."

With respect to my historical sources, you're going to see more than a few references to *The Oxford Companion to Spirits and Cocktails*, edited by David Wondrich and Noah Rothbaum and published in 2021. It is an amazing resource; I recommend you add it to your library. And you're also going to see numerous other references to my old friend David Wondrich, the undisputed dean of cocktail historians.

Lastly, as an aside, I would be remiss if I did not tell you about another amazing resource, the Vintage Cocktail Books Free Digital Library (euvslibrary.com), operated by the Exposition Universelle des Vins et Spiritueux (EUVS). This is the online extension of a museum created by Paul Ricard on Bendor Island in the South of France, where you can view vintage cocktail books going back to the nineteenth century. Truthfully, I can't imagine writing the cocktail books I've written without this incredible collection. To a cocktail geek like me, it's like being a kid in a candy store.

BAR TOOLS AND BASIC INGREDIENTS

YOU CANNOT MAKE A good drink without a good set of bar tools and some basic ingredients, such as syrups, cordials, and other "mixers." Here are a few recommendations.

bar tools and techniques

The Shaker

There are two basic kinds of shakers: the cobbler shaker and the Boston shaker. The cobbler shaker has three pieces: a shaker tin, a strainer, and a cap that sits atop the strainer. A Boston shaker is a simpler affair, consisting of either two metal shaker tins or a metal tin and a pint glass, or "mixing glass." Whether the Boston shaker is all metal or metal and glass, one component is slightly smaller than the other so that the rim of one fits within the rim of the other, to make a tight seal. Professional bartenders tend to use the Boston shaker, but a good cobbler shaker is just fine for home use.

The Stirring Spoon or Barspoon

This long-handled spoon, usually made of metal, is used for stirring a cocktail or adding a float to the top of a drink (see page 5). The good ones have a smooth, spiraled shaft that won't cause a lot of friction when you stir a drink vigorously—we don't want calloused fingers, do we?

When you stir a drink, gently hold the spoon between your middle two fingers at the middle of its shaft. This way, when you stir the drink, the spoon isn't so much *churning through the ice* as *moving the ice in a rotation* around the inside of the mixing glass. In truth, most of the drinks in this book are going to be shaken (as one does with drinks with citrus ingredients), but you're going to need a good spoon to stir drinks whenever there is a fizzy component added after the shaking (such as a Moscow Mule, page 156; or a Tom Collins, page 214).

The Channel Knife and Y-Peeler

To create twists or peels to use as a garnish, you need either a channel knife or a Y-peeler. The channel knife creates a narrow strip of peel, which you might use to garnish your French 75 (page 94). A Y-peeler resembles a slingshot, and makes a wider peel (which I prefer, since it also allows you

This is a common question: Am I to shake a drink or stir a drink, and when do I do which? We've all become accustomed to folks adopting a James Bondian air, wanting a drink "shaken, not stirred." Here's a rule of thumb, which you're welcome to ignore: *shake* a drink that is going to be opaque or cloudy (which is every single drink in this book, since they all contain citrus fruit), but *stir* a drink that's going to end up (relatively) clear.

Also look into the "Regal Shake" or "Regal Stir" method, believed to have been invented either by Theo Lieberman around 2010 at Milk & Honey or Lantern's Keep in New York City. It entails putting a citrus peel (or wedge) into whatever drink you're making and then shaking or stirring the drink. The process of shaking or stirring extracts the oils from the peel to add a new dimension of flavor to your drink. Especially consider Theo's Regal Daiquiri, where he places a grapefruit peel in the shaker.

to express the oils in the peel over the top of your drink). When used correctly, either one will give you a nice thin piece of peel without going deep enough into the skin of the fruit to yield any of its white albedo (often called pith), which can add an unpleasant bitterness to your drink.

The Muddler

Typically made of wood or plastic, a muddler is essential to so many drinks. It's used to mash down ingredients like mint and basil leaves or lime and lemon halves, and by pressing them to express their oils or juices. For example, you'd use a muddler to press the juice and oils out of lime wedges in a Caipirinha or Caipiroska (page 56), or the flavor from basil leaves in a Basil Gin Smash (page 237).

The Swizzle Stick

Not to be confused with the plastic freebie things that might have *accidentally* ended up in your pocket or purse from that swanky hotel bar you went to (that's a "stir stick," by the way), the swizzle stick is a wood or plastic device that resembles a propeller at the end of a long rod. Historically, a swizzle stick was cut from a shrub where a larger branch had branched out into three to five smaller ones. You insert a swizzle stick into the container holding the drink (typically one with crushed ice, such as the Queen's Park Swizzle, page 188) and rub your palms together to twist the swizzle back and forth. It works like a crude little blender, mixing the drink and also chilling it faster.

The Dry Shake

Drinks such as the Pisco Sour (page 182) or Strawberry Daze (page 208) call for a "dry shake," which means you give the drink a vigorous shaking for about 15 seconds *before* adding ice, and then you shake the drink again *after* the ice has been added. The dry shake is often used when a drink calls for egg white or aquafaba (see "What About Egg Whites?" page 10), the theory being that shaking it well without ice allows the egg white to develop a nice foamy texture. Some bartenders do the dry shake before adding ice, some do it after, and some do it before *and* after. And some, such as Jeffrey Morgenthaler (see his famous Amaretto Sour, page 34), eschews the dry shake for an immersion blender.

Topping a Drink

Some drink recipes, such as the Gin Fizz (page 102) and the French 75 (page 94) have you "top" the drink after shaking the noncarbonated ingredients. It simply means you're adding a fizzy component (soda water, Champagne, cola, etc.) to the top of the drink. You typically stir the drink after you add the bubbly ingredient, since you want to mix it into the rest of the drink. You also typically don't want to shake the bubbly component: It will lose its effervescence in the process, not to mention cause the shaker to pop open (and make a mess!) from the force of the release of the bubbles. (It would be like shaking up a can of soda and then opening it.) That said, historically the Ramos Gin Fizz (page 104) was shaken *with* the soda water in it; ol' Henry Ramos simply made sure the shaker had a very tight seal.

Rinsing a Glass

To rinse a glass simply means adding a small amount of a specified liquid to the glass and swirling it around to coat the inside of the glass. For example, when making a classic Sazerac cocktail, you first rinse the inside of your glass with absinthe or anise.

Rinsing a Shaker, or the "Shaker Rinse"

This is a technique I figured out and named on my own; I'm not claiming to have invented it, since it's pretty commonsensical. If you were to make, say, a Daiquiri, there's a pretty good chance that after shaking the rum, lime juice, and sugar or simple syrup for a good 20 seconds, you'll end up with a *very* cold, even frosty shaker, and at least some of the drink's contents still clinging to the ice. If you were then to strain your drink and walk away, you'd be leaving (and wasting) a lot of flavor inside the shaker, still clinging to that ice. So, if you're making, say, a Mojito (page 154), and I ask you to rinse your shaker with soda water, then strain it into the drink, you'll be a) chilling your soda water with the ice that's remaining in the shaker, and b) releasing all that flavor clinging to the ice and adding that goodness to the drink.

The Float and the Sink

Adding a "float" to a drink simply means you're adding a final ingredient that will sit atop the drink; a "sink" is an ingredient that will gently sink down into the drink. These techniques are different from topping a drink since you don't stir a float or a sink; instead, you want the ingredient to either rest atop the drink or seep down the sides for visual effect. To add a float, gently pour the ingredient over the back of a barspoon onto the top of the drink; the spoon encourages it to stay topside. To add a sink, dispense with the spoon so the ingredient is more likely to sink down into the drink.

essential ingredients

Syrups

All the drinks in this book contain a "sweet" component. Sometimes the sweetness comes from a liqueur (see the Margarita, page 140; and the Sidecar, page 200). Often it's from a syrup or cordial. Many of the latter you can make at home, but there are some fine products on the market, which I've suggested in the entries below. Learning to use these different ingredients will help you tailor your drinks to your taste and purposes.

Simple Syrup

It's called "simple syrup" because it is: a syrup simply made with sugar and water. And while you don't need to heat the mixture, you certainly can. The easiest method is to combine sugar and water in a bottle and then stir or shake it; the sugar will eventually dissolve. But if you want to heat it in a saucepan over low heat to speed up the process, please do. Either way, this simple syrup will keep in an airtight bottle or container in the refrigerator for a few weeks.

When making your own simple syrup, you'll likely want to use equal parts water and sugar. Note that where a recipe directs you to use simple syrup, it's going to be a 1:1 ratio unless otherwise specified. When a recipe calls for a "rich simple syrup" or "rock candy syrup," this means a higher percentage of sugar, usually a 1:2 ratio of water to sugar. If you don't like very sweet drinks, or if you're calorie-conscious or prediabetic, just increase the ratio of water to sweetener; some bartenders even prefer a 2:1 ratio of water to sugar.

Brown Sugar Syrup or Demerara Syrup

The method here is the same as for simple syrup, just using brown sugar or Demerara sugar instead of granulated sugar, in the ratio you prefer. Similar to making simple syrup, if you want to heat it in a saucepan over low heat to speed things along, go for it. Like simple syrup, it will keep in an airtight bottle or container in the refrigerator for a few weeks.

Honey Syrup

This also is prepared with the same method as simple syrup, using equal parts honey and water. (Here, heating is recommended as it aids in the dissolution of the honey.) And also like those syrups, it will keep in an airtight bottle or container in the refrigerator for a few weeks.

Cinnamon Syrup

For this syrup, you need to heat the mixture to extract the flavor from the cinnamon sticks. To make about 12 ounces cinnamon syrup, in a medium saucepan, combine 1 cup water, 1 cup sugar, and 2 (6-inch) cinnamon sticks. Bring to a simmer over low heat and cook, stirring occasionally, until the sugar has dissolved, about 10 minutes. Let cool completely. If you want a subtle cinnamon flavor, strain the syrup into an airtight bottle or container and seal. If you want a strong cinnamon flavor, let it sit for a few hours or overnight before straining. The syrup will keep in the refrigerator for up to 1 month.

Pineapple Syrup

Peel and core a whole pineapple, then cut the fruit into chunks. Put the pineapple in a large bowl, add 1 cup sugar, and toss to coat. Cover and refrigerate overnight. The next day, combine 1 cup sugar and 1 cup water in a small saucepan. Bring to a boil over medium heat, stirring until the sugar has dissolved. Remove the pan from the heat. In a blender, puree the macerated pineapple, then add the simple syrup and blend again to combine. Strain the mixture through cheesecloth into a container with a lid and discard the solids; you should have about 15 ounces pineapple syrup. The syrup will keep in the refrigerator for several weeks.

Ginger Syrup

There are a few ways to skin this cat, so to speak. You can use an electric juicer to extract the juice from the ginger and add that to simple syrup, or you can use a trick from Derek Brown's 2022 book *Mindful Mixology: A Comprehensive Guide to No- and Low-Alcohol Cocktails.* See, Derek keeps the ginger in the freezer, and when he wants to make ginger syrup, he simply uses a grater to grate whatever amount he needs, peel and all. It's so much easier doing it this way, as easy as grating Parmesan cheese. Here's his formula: In a small or medium saucepan, combine 1 cup sugar and 1 cup water and bring to a boil over medium-high heat, stirring until the sugar has dissolved. Remove from the heat and add 2 tablespoons grated unpeeled fresh ginger. Let cool, then add a dash of fresh lemon juice, stir, and strain. Transfer to an airtight container or bottle and store in the refrigerator. It will keep for several weeks.

Grenadine

Many of the recipes in this book call for grenadine, such as the Bacardí Cocktail (page 38) and the Jack Rose (page 114). Just as I want you to avoid artificially flavored and colored products (looking at *you*, Rose's Sweetened Lime Juice), I also want you to shun the brands of grenadine found in most grocery stores. How to tell the difference? Easy—just choose a grenadine that is flavored and colored with real pomegranate juice. You do *not* want artificial flavoring, coloring, or high-fructose corn syrup in your grenadine. Stirrings makes a fine grenadine, as do Luxardo and Small Hand Foods.

That said, you can also make your own grenadine by adding some sugar or simple syrup to pomegranate juice in the ratio you prefer, shaking or stirring them until well blended. My homemade grenadine has a 4:1 ratio of juice to simple syrup. I like using POM brand pomegranate juice, which is readily available.

Orgeat

Pronounced *oar-JHAT* (rhymes with "yacht"), orgeat is an almond-flavored syrup. You can search recipes online to make your own, or use a commercial brand (one made with real almond flavoring). My favorite orgeat is from Small Hand Foods, while BG Reynolds and Monin are also very good.

Falernum

This can be either a flavored liqueur or a nonalcoholic syrup. You'll find it in many Caribbean or tiki drinks; tiki pioneer Donn "Don the Beachcomber" Beach likely introduced falernum to American drinkers at his iconic chain of tiki bars back in the 1930s. Originating in the Barbados in the nineteenth century, falernum then was a low-alcohol liqueur made with rum, sugar, and lime juice, with island spices such as cloves, ginger, and nutmeg, and sometimes almonds. (Indeed, you could even call it a bottled Sour.) Today, John D. Taylor's Velvet Falernum is the gold standard among alcoholic versions. BroVo Spirits of Portland, Oregon, also makes a good one. Among the nonalcoholic syrups, I like BG Reynolds and The Bitter Truth.

Lime Cordial

Several drinks in this book call for a lime cordial, such as the Gimlet (page 99) and the Suffering Bastard (page 209). Historically, the primary option in this field has been Rose's Lime Juice Cordial, now known as Rose's Sweetened Lime Juice. (As I've noted, I don't recommend this brand.) But now you can make your own lime cordial, or you can purchase some very fine brands such as Twisted Alchemy's Lime Sour. Also, Fresh Victor makes a bottled Mexican Lime & Agave that's tremendous in a Margarita (page 140), Gimlet (page 99), or anything else calling for lime cordial or sour mix.

Many drink recipes call for the use of egg whites (see the Clover Club, page 64; the Pisco Sour, page 182; and the Ramos Gin Fizz, page 104). However, you might be averse to using egg whites for dietary reasons or due to allergy concerns, or because raw egg can carry the risk of salmonella or other bacteria. So, what to do? Try pasteurized egg whites, sold by the carton. Or you can use something called aquafaba, which is nothing more than the liquid from a can of chickpeas. It's relatively flavorless and imparts a similar foamy texture to your drink. And if you don't want to open a can of chickpeas each time you make a Ramos, there are commercial offerings of aquafaba, notably Fee Brothers' Fee Foam.

To make your own, I offer to you the recipe found David Alan's *Tipsy Texan: Spirits and Cocktails from the Lone Star State*. Here's a condensed version of that recipe: Soak 6 limes in warm water to cover for at least 10 minutes to remove any wax coating, then drain them and allow to dry. Put ¾ cup sugar in a small bowl, then zest the limes over the sugar, making sure not to scrape off any of the bitter white albedo (pith). Cut the zested limes in half and use a handheld juicer to squeeze their juice into the bowl. Stir the mixture very well until it forms a syrup. Cover the bowl and refrigerate for 6 to 8 hours. Strain the syrup, discarding the solids, and transfer to a clean airtight bottle. Seal and store in the refrigerator. It will keep for about 1 month. This recipe makes about 9 ounces of lime cordial.

Another excellent (albeit salty!) lime cordial is found in the recipe for the Far East Gimlet (page 83), by my friend Naren Young.

Fassionola

This is a term for any red-colored fruit syrup, and dates back about one hundred years (if its somewhat murky history can be relied upon). Usually passion fruit–based, fassionola is also known as Passionola and Passiflora.

It was popular at tiki bars, such as Don the Beachcomber's, from the 1930s onward. While several good commercial brands are available, I also include a recipe within the discussion of the Color of Law cocktail (page 66).

Commercial Brands of Cordials, Shrubs, and Syrups, Generally

Just as with grocery store maraschino cherries and certain brands of bottled cordials and syrups, I encourage you to avoid anything that is artificially flavored, sweetened, or colored. Check the label to ensure that the flavor comes from whatever fruit or nut or extract the syrup is supposed to be from. Some fine commercial offerings are available, notably Monin, Giffard, Small Hand Foods, SOM Cordial, Shaker & Spoon, Liber & Co., Pratt Standard, BG Reynolds, Jack Rudy, Stirrings, Liquid Alchemist, Krakus (from Poland), Lowicz (also from Poland), d'arbo, Portland, Routin 1883, AquaRiva, and Fruitful. Also, be sure to check out specialty markets, such as Polish or Middle Eastern markets, for syrups made with fruits not found in mainstream markets. For folks down under, check out the fine offerings of the Simple Syrup Co. for any of your syrup needs. In the United Kingdom, the Bristol Syrup Company is very good.

As a final word on syrups: If you cannot find an obscure syrup—for example, a good groseille syrup (made with red currants)—it's okay to use grenadine, raspberry syrup, or another quality fruit syrup as a replacement; you do need a syrup's sweetness. While the end result won't be the exact same drink, I'm sure it'll still be delicious.

Commercial Juices

If you don't want to squeeze your own lemon, lime, grapefruit, or other kind of fruit juice, there are some fine products out there, including Fresh Victor, Ripe Bar Juice, and Twisted Alchemy. Seek them out, especially brands that are cold-pressed and 100% juice, especially if you're hosting a large gathering or going on a vacation where many drinks will be made. The brands mentioned also offer some good-quality juice-based cocktail mixes. There are also some excellent pureed juices like Coco Reàl's line of products such as coconut, for making a Painkiller (page 165), and Perfect Puree, if you're making a strawberry- or other fruit-flavored Daiquiri (page 75).

Oleo Citrate and "Super Juice"

No, this isn't some sort of genetically modified hybrid of lemon, lime, and grapefruit; it's nothing more than an ingenious method of extracting as much flavor as possible from one piece of fruit. Think of it: when you juice a lime, you're extracting about an ounce-plus of lime juice and tossing away the rest. Very wasteful, no? Well, Nickle Morris, a bartender and co-owner of cocktail bar Expo in Louisville, Kentucky, came up with a way to not only increase the yield from the fruit but also increase the yield's stability and shelf life. The term "oleo citrate" refers to essential oils extracted from citrus peel, and Super Juice is the result when you add juice and water to those oils.

How? The answer lies in the fact that there's a lot of flavor in the outer layer of the peel, the flavedo or "zest." (Important: The zest is the colored outer peel, not the bitter white part, which is called the albedo, or pith.) By extracting flavor from the zest, stabilizing it with citric and malic acid, then adding water to the mixture to dilute and extend it, you can get a lot more out of each piece of fruit.

Using this process, you'll end up with about 45 ounces of lime oleo citrate or Super Juice from 10 limes or 8 lemons, which otherwise would have yielded only 8 to 10 ounces of citrus juice. Here's how: Using a Y-peeler, peel 10 limes or 8 lemons, being careful to remove only the colorful flavedo (zest) and leaving behind the bitter white albedo (pith); you'll need 3½ ounces of peel. Set aside the peeled fruits. Place the peels in a clean container, then add 1½ ounces powdered citric acid and ¼ ounce powdered malic acid. Shake or toss the peels and acids together, enough to ensure that the acids fully come into contact with the peels. Set aside at room temperature, uncovered, for about 1 hour. Add 34 ounces (4¼ cups) water and, using an immersion blender, blend well. (You can vary the amount of water to reduce or increase the yield to taste.) Strain the mixture through cheesecloth or a fine-mesh strainer and discard the solids. Juice the peeled fruits and add the juice to the strained mixture. Transfer to a clean, airtight bottle. Seal and store in the refrigerator. It should keep for several weeks.

Other Juices

Most of the drinks in this book are made with either lemon or lime juice since those fruits have been the main sour components in a bartender's toolkit from the earliest days of punch, around 1638. While Eureka lemons and Persian limes are the standard varieties you'll find in most grocery stores and produce markets, don't let that limit you. Indeed, if you look around, you'll see there's a whole wide world of other citrus fruits that can help you to expand your options when it comes to making delicious sour-based cocktails. For example, there are more drinks being made with yuzu juice, such as the Six-Toed Cat (see page 78) and the Far East Gimlet (page 83). Yuzu is a delightful citrus fruit from East Asia (including China, Korea, and Japan), the juice of which reminds me of a cross between lemon and tangerine, very floral and tart. Yuzu fruits from Asia and Australia cannot be imported into the United States; however, it is now cultivated in the southern US, and it's easily available online. I've had great success with the bottled yuzu juice from Yuzuco and Yakami Orchard. Of course, if you're adventurous, you can order a yuzu tree and grow your own fruits!

While we're on the topic of the rising popularity of yuzu juice, note that one of my favorite orange curaçaos, Ferrand Dry Curaçao, recently launched their new Late Harvest Limited Edition, flavored with yuzu. It's delightful—try it in your next Margarita (page 140) or Sidecar (page 200).

You may also be seeing more cocktails made with satsuma, mandarin, bitter orange, tomate de árbol (also known as tamarillo), sudachi, kabosu, calamansi, makrut lime, Meyer lemon, key lime, finger lime, and loquat juice. While many of these fruits are not available in their fresh forms (due to import controls), you can find them as bottled juices. Reliable sources include Yakami Orchard and International Gourmet Foods, or check out international markets in your area for bottled juices.

Hydrosols and Aromatic Mists

Think of hydrosols as superconcentrated flavor compounds made from the distillation of the essential oils of a plant, flower, or other botanical offering. Rose water and orange flower water are good examples, the latter of which is essential in a Ramos Gin Fizz (page 104). A number of companies, like Bluestem Botanicals, offer products such as basil hydrosol, thyme-rosemary hydrosol, and others. Aromatic cocktail mists allow you to easily impart scents with orange oil, grapefruit oil, or lemon oil. Some of these combine essences and scents, like grapefruit and coriander, lemon and star anise, and mint and grapefruit. Shaker & Spoon is a good source for these.

Commercial Cocktail Kits

Many companies now offer kits containing everything you need to make a great drink, from the spirit(s) and fresh fruit (or bottled juices) to the syrups and the spiced salt or sugar for the rim. Note that depending on your state's regulations on the shipping of alcoholic beverages, there may be limitations on what you can purchase in these kits; for example, you may need to buy the spirit separately but purchase everything else in a kit. Check out Cocktail Courier, Shaker & Spoon, SaloonBox, The Cocktail Box Co., American Cocktail Club, and Crafted Taste. Some of these companies occupy certain niches in the marketplace, like Haus, which offers products with a lower-alcohol and apéritif bent to them, and Shaker & Spoon, which sets you up with a range of subscription options that are great for gifting.

Garnishes

CHERRIES

When I refer to "cocktail cherries," I'm not talking about the little jars of cherries that you find in most grocery stores. These are to be avoided, as they're artificially flavored and colored. No, spend a little more and get some "gourmet" cocktail cherries from brands like Luxardo, Amarena

Fabbri, and Traverse City Whiskey Co. instead. Why waste the effort of a finely crafted cocktail with a bad garnish? You deserve better.

SALTS, SUGARS, AND OTHER GARNISHES

Okay, we all know that the glass for a Sidecar has a sugar-encrusted rim, while the rim of a margarita glass gets a coating of coarse salt. But let's not stop there! There are so many other great garnish options that you can either make at home or purchase online. For example, Shaker & Spoon has a tremendous variety, including Sother's Hibiscus Salt, Lemongrass Salt, Cinnamon Spiced Sugar, and, for that Bloody Mary, some spicy Cayenne Salt. Also check out Jacobsen Salt Co., iGourmet.com, Shaker & Spoon, Desert Provisions, Lava Craft Cocktail Co., Rokz, Collins Consumables, Lava, and the Spice Lab. Or do a little research and experimenting on your own to figure out how to make these kinds of garnishes at home, particularly since their shelf lives will be fairly long.

Look into the range of garnishes, from dehydrated lemon wheels to peels and twists packed in flavored syrups to candied ginger (essential for the Penicillin, page 174). Worthy purveyors include WebRestaurantStore.com, CollinsChicago.com, Twisted Alchemy, and many others.

A Final Note on Brands

In this book, when I offer a recipe either created by a contemporary bartender or found in a vintage bartending book, I call for the specific brand(s) indicated in the original. I do this to be faithful to the original recipe and its author or the drink's creator. Many bartenders and drinks writers are precise (if not fussy) about what brands they use in their cocktails, perhaps because they've made an extensive investment of time and energy in finding the right brand, or because they have a contractual relationship with a particular brand or serve as a brand ambassador. But don't feel compelled to use the same brand to make a great cocktail—if you have a preferred substitute or want to use what you have on hand, do so. Use common sense and you'll be fine.

THE SOUR COCKTAIL: ORIGINS

OR, A (VERY) BRIEF OVERVIEW OF MANKIND'S ENJOYMENT OF ALCOHOLIC BEVERAGES, AND THE EVOLUTION OF THE SOUR

"Civilization begins with distillation."
—AMERICAN NOVELIST WILLIAM FAULKNER (1897–1962)

People have been consuming alcoholic beverages for thousands of years. Beer (a fermented grain beverage), wine (fermented grape juice), mead (a fermented honey beverage), and cider (fermented juice from tree fruits) were among the original alcoholic beverages. There are many, many references across ancient literature and history about fermented beverages. In the New Testament, after all, Jesus magically transformed water into wine when they'd run out of the stuff at the Wedding at Cana. Good guy to have around, that Jesus.

A "fermented" beverage starts out as a nonalcoholic drink (such as grape juice); when yeast is added to it, a chemical reaction takes place. The yeast devours the sugars in the juice, and the by-product is ethyl alcohol or, in this case, wine, a fermented form of the original juice that is approximately 10 to 14 percent alcohol. Pretty low-proof, all things considered.

So, how did our earliest ancestors figure all this out? It's believed that some if not all of these types of beverages were happy accidents, whereby naturally occurring, airborne yeasts interacted with fruit or juice. This sort of thing still happens today. (If you don't believe me, google "birds eating fermented berries." You're welcome.)

Okay, that's fermentation, so what's *distillation*? Distillation is a process whereby the water is removed from a fermented beverage (like that wine we just made), resulting in a very concentrated (and more potent) version of the original beverage. Distilled wine or other fruit juices is called brandy. Distilled beer is called whisk(e)y. If you make a "wine" of sugarcane juice and then distill it, it's rum.

So how does distillation work? Well, you know what happens when you put a pot of water on the stove and turn the heat up to high? How the water boils and turns into a vapor, or "spirit"? Same thing. But it has to be done with precision; after all, if you simply "boil" wine, won't the vapor escape?

Ah, that's where the science and the method come in. You see, alcohol and water have different boiling points. Water boils at 212°F (100°C), while the boiling point of alcohol is much lower (173°F/78°C). If you use a contraption called a still, you can heat the wine up to about 175°F (79.4°C), which turns the alcohol in the wine into a vapor. The vapor cools and turns back into a liquid, a distilled spirit. What happens next depends on what you're making. If you're making bourbon, you start with a fermented corn "mash" (kind of like beer), and it must spend a certain amount of time in charred white oak barrels before it can be called bourbon. Cognac and Armagnac (distilled wines from certain grapes from certain regions of France) will also spend time in oak barrels. But other distilled spirits can be consumed right off the still, such as vodka, light rum, gin, and moonshine, where (generally) no aging in wood (or other) vessels is required.

So that's how wine is made. From there you have fortified wines (such as vermouth, sherry, port, Marsala, and Madeira), which are regular wines to which a distilled wine (brandy) is introduced to "fortify" it and improve its taste and longevity; liqueurs (alcoholic beverages containing a wide range of flavorings, from botanicals to herbs and roots and blossoms); to amari and bitter apéritifs (similar to fortified wines but usually with a more bitter flavor profile); and so on.

These are the "usual suspects" in the "strong" portion of our Sour cocktails.

enter citrus, and the reign of punch

Like fermented beverages, the juices of citrus fruits have been enjoyed as beverages for many centuries. And they've played a significant role in the making of what we'd now call "mixed drinks" for nearly that long. For example, during the reign of France's Sun King, Louis XIV (1651–1715), a profession known as the limonadiers rose in popularity. Per *Eating the Enlightenment: Food and the Sciences in Paris, 1670–1760*, these were merchants engaged in "the preparation and sale of a variety of hot and cold beverages, ices, and preserved fruits and nuts." The first official guild of limonadiers, "the guild of 'Master Distillers of brandy, & of all other waters, & Merchants of brandy, & of all kinds of liqueurs,'" was established in France in 1676. Testament to the popularity of citrus and other fruits in the drinking habits of France from the seventeenth century onward, the term *limonadier* was defined in 1690 (in *The Universal Dictionary* by Antoine Furetière) as "un Marchand qui vend de la lemonade, de la liqueur et plusiers autres sortes de liqueur, comme eaux de cerises, verjus, groseilles, framboise, du sorbet, de l'orangeade, etc." ("a merchant who sells hard lemonade, and many other types of liqueurs, such as cherry, verjus [the juice of unripened grapes], red currant, raspberry, sorbet, orangeade, etc.").

Among the earliest references to citrus joining forces with strong drink is in a tract written by an Englishman named George Gascoigne in 1576. Its title alone has a certain "Damn, I've hit rock bottom with alla mah boozin'" tone to it. To wit: *A Delicate Diet for Daintiemouthde Droonkardes; Wherein the Fowle Abuse of Common Carowsing, and Quaffing with Hartie Draughtes, Is Honestlie Admonished.* Within this epic tome comes Gascoigne's chagrined resignation that while drinkers of the day had a full range of options available, from various beers to wines to ales, you sometimes gots to have the hard stuff: "Yea, wine of itselfe is not sufficient; but Sugar, Limons, and sundry sortes of spices must be drowned therein."

And then you have punch, perhaps the earliest, and certainly the most significant, marriage of sweet, sour, and strong, which cocktail historians such as David Wondrich, author of *Punch: The Desires (and Dangers) of the Flowing Bowl,* confirm was being consumed by British colonials in nineteenth-century India. Great Britain established the East India Company in 1600, which commenced a robust commerce (in commodities such as textiles, dyes, sugar, salt, spices, tea, and opium) with Mother England and other international ports of call from trading posts established in India from 1614 onward. According to *The Oxford Companion to Spirits and Cocktails,* the earliest known reference to punch (by name) came in 1638, when a German traveler, Johann Albrecht von Mandelslo, observed a group of Brits in Surat, India, enjoying "a kind of drink consisting of aqua-vitae, rose-water, juices of citrons and sugar." Another visitor to Surat, circa 1630, wrote of a drink popular among the English traders, consisting of "a Composition of Racke [arrack, a distilled sugarcane and rice spirit made in Indonesia since the 1600s], water, sugar, and Juice of Lymes." In both of these references we can plainly see the marriage of our three core ingredients in the Sour platform of drinks: something sweet, something strong, and something sour.

The Oxford Companion defines "punch" as "a mixture of spirits, citrus juice, sugar, and water, often with the addition of spices," and "is the foundational drink of modern mixology and the first mixed drink based on spirits to gain global popularity." By virtue of being a popular drink in British-occupied India, which in turn was a vital trading port and point of departure for a vast array of spices, flavorings, foods, and beverages, it's no mystery that the drink soon became popular worldwide, establishing itself as a staple in the Caribbean, North America, and the British Isles by the 1660s.

It's interesting to note that the role played by citrus fruits in punch wasn't limited to just the juice. As early as the seventeenth century, oleosaccharum ("sugared oil" in Latin) was an ingredient in punch recipes. Oleosaccharum is the result of a maceration process, using sugar to draw out the flavorful oils from the outer peel, or flavedo (often called the zest), of a fruit. An essential part of the punch, it was an ingenious and resourceful use of the seemingly extraneous peel, adding flavor, bitterness, and sweetness to the drink. Oleosaccharum has made something of a comeback in the past fifteen or so years among bartenders and cocktail enthusiasts. You can also see a modern-day application of this ingenuity in the discussion of oleo citrate and "Super Juice" (page 12).

the rise of the cocktail and the individualized drink

But punch was, and still is, a communal, one-size-fits-all drink. (It's served in a big ol' punch bowl, right?) Fast-forward to the end of the eighteenth century, after the fledgling United States had declared its independence from Great Britain and just enjoyed the first two terms in office of its first president, George Washington (himself a distiller and drinkin' man). That's when "single-size" drinks began to cater to the individual.

See, the whole social construct of partaking of punch required an investment of considerable time. Think of a poker game, or a round of golf with friends. One does not leave the table after a few hands (sorry, Kenny Rogers), or cut out on one's foursome after six holes. That would be rude.

No, the consumption of punch required a commitment to however many hours it took to "fathom the bowl" and render it dry, a group effort. Then, as David Wondrich puts it in his book *Imbibe!*,

> As the eighteenth century wore into the nineteenth, that time was less and less likely to be there. Industrialization, improved communications, and the rise of the bourgeoisie all made claims on the individual that militated against partaking of the Flowing Bowl. . . . It's not that Americans suddenly stopped liking punch. But they were busy, or at least thought it a virtue to seem that way. To sit around in a tavern ladling libations out of a capacious bowl was as much to confess that you didn't have anywhere to be for the next few hours, and America was a go-ahead country, as everyone was always saying.

Around this time we began to see the rise of individual drinks, known as *cocktails*. After all, while punch might be a marathon, the cocktail is a sprint.

Indeed, drink historians begin to see references to "cock-tails" in the 1790s, with the term defined in print for the first time in 1806. That definition was published in a newspaper based in Hudson, New York, called *Balance and Columbian Repository*: "a stimulating liquor, composed of spirits of any kind, sugar water and bitters—it is vulgarly called a bittered sling, and is supposed to be an excellent electioneering potion inasmuch as it renders the heart stout and bold, at the same time that it fuddles the head. It is said also, to be of great use to a democratic candidate: because, a person having swallowed a glass of it, is ready to swallow anything else." Politics aside, the dawn of the day of the individual drink had arrived.

Of course, when you've had nearly three centuries of delicious libations "consisting of aqua-vitae, rose-water, juices of citrons and sugar," you don't just throw out all those great punch recipes because you want to make single-sized drinks. No, you simply "downsize" some of those great punches. That idea is what ultimately spawned what Wondrich refers to as "The Children of Punch," including the Sour cocktail.

the 1850s: enter the crusta, the fix, and the sour, and the first cocktail recipes

The middle part of the nineteenth century saw three profound developments in the bartending world—and these developments took place many miles apart: the earliest-known reference to the "Sour" and "Fix" cocktails; the creation of the "Crusta" style of cocktail; and the publication of the world's first cocktail recipe book. Let's take them one at a time.

We begin in a saloon in Toronto, Canada, called Mart Ackermann's, whose beverage program appeared to be top-notch. Their "Bill of Fare" (or drinks menu, with the date "1856" written on the cover), listed a wide range of cocktails and mixed drinks, including thirty-five kinds of punches and fifteen different cobblers; of significance to this discussion are seven Fixes and two Sours—the earliest-known reference to these styles of drinks.

The following year saw the earliest-known reference to the Sour cocktail within a newspaper: a June 23, 1857 *New York Times* article that cheekily referred to William J. Brisley, a New York City alderman, as "Brandy-sour Brisley." This reference, combined with the Ackermann's menu, suggests that the Sour was firmly on the map by the mid-1850s.

Meanwhile, way down yonder in New Orleans, the 1850s also saw the birth of a category of drink that was quite possibly instrumental in launching the Sour. (Or perhaps it wasn't, as we'll come to see.) There, an Italian immigrant by the name of Joseph Santini ran the bar at the New Orleans City Exchange (within the historic St. Louis Hotel, which occupied the city block of St. Louis Street, between Chartres and Royal in the French Quarter) and later opened his own bar, the Jewel of the South, on Gravier Street near the St. Charles Hotel. At one of these two establishments, Santini created a category of drink called the Crusta, which may have been the progenitor of the Sour cocktail. More on that momentarily.

The third momentous event came in 1862, with the publication of the earliest-known cocktail book, *The Bar-Tenders' Guide: A Complete Cyclopedia of Plain and Fancy Drinks*. Within this epic tome, its author, bartender Jerry Thomas, offered a chapter on "Fixes and Sours," with recipes for the Brandy Fix, the Gin Fix, the Brandy Sour, and the Gin Sour. Clearly, the Sour and the Fix were on the map.

In his *Oxford Companion* article on the Sour, Wondrich further explains that the increasing popularity of the Sour cocktail led to the development of a new (and larger) style of stemmed cocktail glass to accommodate the slightly larger drink. In fact, whereas the original Brandy Cocktail, for example, would have only brandy, bitters, a little water, and some sugar, the Sour was larger due to the inclusion of juice.

It's up for debate which came first, the Fix or the Sour; they're both essentially the same drink, but with the Fix having a fancy garnish of whatever fruit was in season. At Ackermann's saloon, one could order a Brandy Fix, a Gin Fix, a Sherry Fix, a Port Wine Fix, a Cherry Brandy Fix, an Old Tom Fix, a Ladies' Fancy Fix, a Brandy Sour, and a Gin Sour—all presumably drinks with the specified spirit as the base, some form of citrus (likely lemon), and a sweetener (likely gum or gomme syrup).

But let's get back to our friend Santini and his Crusta. In *The Bar-Tenders' Guide*, Thomas actually mentioned Santini by name (sort of—he called him "Santina"), and offered no fewer than five of Santini's drinks, more than any other bartender in the book. In addition to Santini's Pousse Café (brandy, maraschino, and "curaçoa," which was how curaçao was spelled back in the day) and his Dry Punch (brandy, water, tea, Jamaica rum, curaçao, lemon juice, and sugar), Thomas offered three versions of an invention that some cocktail historians believe to be either the father of the Sour, the progenitor of the Sidecar, or both. That would be the Crusta—in particular, the Brandy Crusta. The drink combined brandy, sugar, ice, and "a little lemon juice," served in a goblet with its rim crusted (hence the name) with "pulverized white sugar" and garnished with a large lemon peel. Also offered were a Whiskey Crusta and a Gin Crusta, the same drink but with a different spirit.

Was the Crusta the father of the Sour cocktail, as well as the immortal Sidecar? Or was there not enough lemon juice to qualify for either? It's hard to say. Thomas doesn't specify quantity, just the inclusion of "a little lemon juice." If the amount of lemon juice is but an accent to the drink, to "brighten" it up, perhaps not. But if the amount were, say, half an ounce, then we're onto something. But in discussions about the Sidecar (page 200) and the Margarita (page 140), some historians (notably Wondrich) point to the Daisy (page 26) as the progenitor of these two classics, inasmuch as both contain an orange liqueur as the sweetener. Then again, in *The Joy of Mixology*, Gary Regan referred to the Brandy Crusta as "the template for a string of cocktails we know of as New Orleans Sours," and notes, via Wondrich, that it was the first cocktail to include citrus juice.

Which brings us back to that two-part question: Was the Crusta the father of the Sour, and the Brandy Crusta therefore the Sidecar's daddy?

For many years I wanted to believe this theory, but now I'm dubious. Why? Well, when I look back at Jerry Thomas and his *Bar-Tenders' Guide*, what tips the scales for me toward *not* believing it is this: Thomas had a chapter on "The Cocktail and Crusta" *and* a separate chapter on "Fixes and Sours." That should tell you that in the mind of "the Professor" (as Thomas was known), the Brandy Crusta was not a Sour, because it didn't have enough lemon juice and was made in a different style. If it *were* a Sour, would it not be listed within the Fixes and Sours? But like so many topics in cocktail history and folklore, the matter remains open for debate.

drink platforms based on the sweet/sour/strong trinity: a few words on taxonomy

In the decades that led up to Prohibition, a wide range of drink styles based on the "short punch" or Sour platform began to appear in cocktail books and newspaper articles, and on menus.

THE (SIMPLE) SOUR: A drink containing just the three elements of sweet, strong, and sour; notable examples are the Daiquiri (page 75) and Whiskey Sour (page 229), among others.

THE SPARKLING SOUR: A Sour supplemented by a carbonated beverage, such as Champagne or other sparkling wine, or soda water. Examples include the French 75 (page 94) and Mojito (page 154).

THE FIX: A Sour with a fruit garnish, typically raspberries, blackberries, and so on. However, note Gary Regan's take in his *The Joy of Mixology*: A Fix is a Sour sweetened by pineapple juice.

THE FIZZ: A drink containing (at its core) spirits, citrus juice, sugar, and soda water, served up. As we'll see in the discussion of the wide range of Fizzes (see pages 112-113), this platform eventually took on a range of dairy components, from egg to cream (witness the Ramos Gin Fizz, Silver Fizz, Golden Fizz, and others).

THE COLLINS: A drink containing spirits, citrus juice (usually lemon, although a Rum Collins typically calls for lime), sugar, and soda water, served on the rocks (see the Tom Collins et al., page 214). Among the older categories of drinks that survive today, the Collins is believed to date back to the gin punch–based drinks made by John Collins (c. 1771–1843), the head waiter and proprietor of Limmer's Old House in London. It's among the styles of drinks catalogued in the 1876 edition of Jerry Thomas's *Bar-Tender's Guide*, like the "Tom Collins Whiskey," "Tom Collins Brandy," and "Tom Collins Gin." It also is known for the "Collins" style of glass, a tall stemless glass holding about 14 ounces.

THE DAISY: Usually a Sour cocktail in which the sweetener is an orange liqueur (as opposed to simple syrup, grenadine, etc.) with a bit of soda water, served in a stemmed cocktail glass. However: Some Daisies contain raspberry syrup as the sweetener, as well as orgeat and Chartreuse (see page 124). Gary Regan, in *The Joy of Mixology*, states that a Daisy is sweetened by grenadine.

THE COOLER: A vague-ish category of drinks containing a spirit, ice, soda water, and often (but not always) citrus. See the Boston Cooler (page 88) and the Florodora (page 87). The original Cooler was the Remsen Cooler, made with a now-defunct brand of Scotch whisky. The defining element of the Cooler is the long lemon peel that serves as a garnish. (Accordingly, David Embury, in his 1948 *The Fine Art of Mixing Drinks*, referred to a Cooler as "essentially a HORSE'S NECK WITH A KICK.") Many coolers lack the required citrus juice to make it into this book; nevertheless, I've included a couple.

THE SWIZZLE: This category has more to do with the method of making the drink than its components. However, many Swizzles have citrus (typically lime juice), spirit (rum is a favorite, also gin), and often bitters. A tall glass is filled with crushed ice, the ingredients are added, and a swizzle stick (see page 4) is inserted and rotated briskly between the palms of the hands, which agitates or "swizzles" the drink.

THE BUCK AND THE MULE: Spirits with lime juice and ginger beer or ale (which serves as the sweetener and fizzy component combined). Examples of this are the Gin Buck, as well as the Moscow Mule (page 156) and Audrey Saunders's modern classic the Gin-Gin Mule. Is a Buck the same as a Mule? Some will argue that a Buck has ginger ale while the Mule has ginger beer, or that a Mule has lime juice while a Buck might have lime or lemon juice.

THE SLING: If the definition found in *The Oxford Companion to Spirits and Cocktails* is to be believed (I question it only because I'm the one who wrote it!), "the sling, a simple, even basic mixture of spirits, sugar, and water, is among the earlier varieties of mixed alcoholic beverage." Some Slings, such as the Straits Sling (page 206, not to be confused with the Singapore Sling), contain citrus.

PUNCH (SINGLE-SERVING, THAT IS): While the term "punch" usually refers to a large-scale beverage served in a punch bowl, there are many single-size versions, including Pisco Punch (page 179), Planter's Punch (page 184), Hurricane (page 107), and the Myrtle Bank Punch (page 160). They all follow the same formula: something sweet, something strong, and something sour as the core.

TWENTY-FIRST-CENTURY SMASHES: A term of my own creation (I think), referring to a style of drink launched by legendary bartender Dale DeGroff circa 1999. He took the original Smash (which in the nineteenth century was simply a smaller version of a Mint Julep), added lemon juice, and started something of a revolution in bartending circles. See the Whiskey Smash and related drinks, page 227.

As a final tip of the hat to Gary Regan, here are a few categories of his own:

INTERNATIONAL SOURS: Sour cocktails wherein the sweet component comes from a liqueur. Examples include the Last Word (page 124), the Aviation (page 36), and the Pegu Club (page 172).

NEW ORLEANS SOURS: Sour cocktails with an orange liqueur as the sweetener, and that (in Regan's mind) descend from the Brandy Crusta (see page viii). Contrast this category, however, with the Daisy (see page 26), not to mention the International Sour. In fact, a New Orleans Sour could be considered a subset of the International Sour.

SQUIRREL SOURS: Sour cocktails that use a nut-based liqueur (such as crème de noyau, Frangelico, or Amaretto) as the sweetener and/or strong component. Examples include the French Squirrel (page 98) and Amaretto Sour (page 34).

ENHANCED SOUR: Spirit, citrus, any sweetener, plus an aromatized and/or fortified wine (such as vermouth or Lillet). Examples include the Scoff-Law (page 196) and the Corpse Reviver No. 2 (page 68).

Some of these categories might make you wonder, "What's the difference between, say, a Collins and a Cooler?" Take, for example, the Boston Cooler (see page 88). It has a spirit, citrus, and simple syrup, and it's served in a tall glass on the rocks with soda water, just like a contemporary Tom Collins, except with rum in place of the gin. So, why isn't the Boston Cooler considered a Collins? Because, smarty-pants, it's a Cooler, that's why.

As a final comment on the whole "what qualifies as what?" discussion, for purposes of this book, my "cutoff" point for considering a drink worthy of inclusion is ⅓ ounce of sour (lemon, lime, or grapefruit juice). Sure, that's arbitrary, but you have to draw the line somewhere. There's a great drink from the Violet Hour in Chicago called the Art of Choke that I strongly recommend you check out; however, because it has less than a teaspoon of lime juice, it didn't make the cut. But a drink based on it, the Folk Art (page 89), *did* make the cut because Sarah Rosner uses a full ½ ounce of lime juice, plus pineapple juice, in her variation.

Are there drinks that are definitely *not* sours but, because of how a certain person might make it, perhaps *could* be? Take, for example, the gin & tonic that James Bond enjoyed in Ian Fleming's 1958 novel *Dr. No*. In one scene, "Bond ordered a double gin and tonic and one whole green lime. When the drink came he cut the lime in half, dropped the two squeezed halves into the long glass, almost filled the glass with ice cubes, and then poured in the tonic. One whole lime is about 1 ounce, so that qualifies, right? The gin is the strong and the tonic water has the sweet, so that's like a Tom Collins Tonic, right? Well, no, sorry, I don't think so. Please do make and enjoy that drink, though! In my mind you cannot have enough lime juice in a G&T, but I'm not going to put it in this book. Oh, right, I just did.

ѕumming up

We're well into the third decade of what's come to be known as the Cocktail Renaissance, and so let's be thankful that today's bartenders are knowledgeable about all of these varieties of drinks, and continue to create new expressions of punch, the Sour, the Fizz, the Collins, the Twenty-First-Century Smash, and so many others. Now, having read this little introduction, you'll be able to walk into a bar, scan the drink menu, and show off your knowledge to your friends about how drinks are made and categorized—and also invent your own delicious spinoffs yourself at home. Cheers!

SOUR COCKTAIL CHART

For those who are more visually oriented, here's a nice little chart showing just a handful of Sour cocktails to show how easy this all can be.

DRINK NAME	STRONG
Whiskey Sour	whiskey
Bee's Knees	gin
Daiquiri	light rum
Margarita	tequila
Sidecar	Cognac/brandy
Pisco Sour	pisco
Cosmopolitan	vodka
Jack Rose	Calvados or applejack/ apple brandy
Mai Tai	dark rum
Tom Collins/ Gin Fizz	gin
Mojito	light rum
French 75	gin (or Cognac, if in New Orleans)

SWEET	SOUR	ADD'L INGRED.
sugar/simple syrup	lemon	egg white (optional)
honey/honey syrup	lemon	-
sugar/simple syrup	lime	-
orange liqueur	lime	-
orange liqueur	lemon	sugar-crusted rim
sugar/simple syrup	lime	egg white, Angostura aromatic bitters
orange liqueur	lime	cranberry juice
grenadine	lime or lemon	-
orgeat syrup and orange curaçao	lime	-
sugar/simple syrup	lemon	soda water
sugar/simple syrup	lime	soda water and mint
sugar/simple syrup	lemon	Champagne

THE DRINKS

AMARETTO SOUR

On February 9, 2012, Portland, Oregon, bartending legend and friend o' mine Jeffrey Morgenthaler posted a very humble and unassuming little article on his website titled "I Make the Best Amaretto Sour in the World." He led off the post with: "No, really. I'm serious. In case you think I'm joking, or that you read that wrong, let me go on the record right now: I make the best Amaretto Sour you've ever had in your life. No ifs, ands, or buts about it, my Amaretto Sour dominates and crushes all others out there. And now, I'm going to share my secrets with you." And that's what he proceeded to do. And you know what? He's right. But first, a little background on the drink that he makes better than anyone. On Earth.

The main ingredient is, of course, amaretto, an almond liqueur that's been made in Saronno, in the Lombardy region of Italy, since the Renaissance. Disaronno Originale is the most famous brand and the industry standard. The original Amaretto Sour, which was composed of two parts amaretto liqueur to one part fresh lemon juice, was introduced by the importer of Disaronno in 1974, and it was one of the more popular drinks of the 1980s. Unfortunately, like many drinks from those dark days of cocktail history, the lemon juice was likely not freshly squeezed; it was probably "sour mix" out of a gun.

Sour mix is a legacy of the Cocktail Dark Ages, roughly 1960 to 2000, when artificial ingredients and mass production reigned supreme and craft was considered passé. It consists of sugar (or some other sweetener) and artificially flavored lemon and/or lime juice, and was de rigueur in bars and restaurants across this great land from the 1960s onward. If you find yourself in a bar that still uses sour mix, especially out of a dispenser gun, run away. *Fast.*

Naturally, you can make your own sour mix at home. Let's say you're serving a lot of whiskey sours to your friends—premix freshly squeezed lemon juice and simple syrup at whatever ratio you want to use, and *bam!* You've just made yourself some sour mix that's actually palatable, *because it's made from real ingredients.* There are also some fine new offerings out there from brands such as Fresh Victor, Ripe Bar Juice, and Twisted Alchemy that contain 100% juice and natural sweeteners (sugar, agave syrup, etc.).

Suffice it to say, the 1980s-era Amaretto Sour was a very sweet drink. Fast-forward to 2012 when Jeffrey, while working as the bar manager at Clyde Common in Portland, Oregon, set about figuring out a way to improve this classic. He decided that the amaretto needed help, and that help would come from cask-strength bourbon whiskey and some egg white. And rather than just dry shaking the ingredients before shaking with ice, he used an immersion blender to really get a good froth going. Here's his recipe, which, in case you forgot, will result in *the best Amaretto Sour you've ever had in your life.*

makes 1 cocktail

1½ ounces amaretto

¾ ounce cask-proof bourbon (Jeffrey likes Booker's)

1 ounce fresh lemon juice

1 teaspoon rich simple syrup (see page 6)

½ ounce egg white, lightly beaten

1 lemon peel, for garnish

3 brandied cherries, for garnish (optional)

Combine the amaretto, bourbon, lemon juice, simple syrup, and egg white in a cocktail shaker and shake without ice, or (even better) use an immersion blender to combine and froth. Add cracked ice and shake again. Strain over fresh ice into an Old-Fashioned glass. Garnish with the lemon peel and brandied cherries, if desired. Then, as Jeffrey instructs, "Serve and grin like an idiot as your friends freak out."

AVIATION

We've all seen it: an event or pop culture phenomenon will happen and someone will invent a drink named after it. You've got the Scoff-Law (page 196), the Monkey Gland (see page 196), the Coronation Cocktail (celebrating King Edward VII's ascension to the British throne), the Spirit of St. Louis (named for the plane piloted by Charles Lindbergh in the first nonstop solo transatlantic flight), and many others. Well, it was December 17, 1903, when Orville and Wilbur Wright succeeded in the first manned flight in Kitty Hawk, North Carolina, and by the 1910s, aviation was becoming quite the thing (similar to how today's billionaires are now dabbling in space flight). And, as is the custom, cocktails named after this new fad became quite popular.

The recipe shown here is not the only pre-Prohibition drink bearing this name. Indeed, the *Omaha Daily News* of May 7, 1911, asked the question, "Have you tried an aviation cocktail?" It went on to define it as "one glass of ice, one dash of grenadine, syrup, absinthe, one jigger of apple brandy, half a lime, shake and strain into a cocktail glass." Hmmm, that actually sounds more like a Jack Rose (page 114) with a dash of absinthe. Also, the *San Francisco Chronicle* of January 9, 1911, offered another "aviation cocktail," but it was actually more like a Manhattan.

Thankfully, there was a better source for the Aviation's true recipe back in the day than the newspapers. Which brings us to Hugo Ensslin, once the head bartender at the Hotel Wallick in New York City. In 1916 he published a tremendous little cocktail book called *Recipes for Mixed Drinks* (an expanded edition would follow in 1917). Ensslin's book contained the earliest-known recipes for several cocktails that have endured the test of time, notably the Blue Moon, the September Morn, and that classic named after mankind's newfound infatuation with flight, the Aviation. Here's how.

1½ ounces London dry gin

½ ounce fresh lemon juice

¼ ounce maraschino liqueur

1 teaspoon Crème Yvette or crème de violette

Combine all the ingredients in a cocktail shaker filled with ice. Shake well, then strain into a chilled cocktail glass.

> **note:** Be careful not to add too much maraschino liqueur or crème de violette, or the drink will taste like hand soap. (That's the opinion of the venerable Dale DeGroff, anyway, and I happen to agree with him! You'll thank me later.)

variation: Delete the maraschino liqueur from the Aviation, and you've got yourself a Blue Moon, a lovely drink to which egg white is added in some versions—a worthy addition. Some of the early twentieth-century recipes for the Blue Moon omit *both* the lemon and the maraschino, and use equal parts gin and crème de violette—but that really sounds like hand soap to me!

BACARDÍ COCKTAIL

This is essentially a Daiquiri (page 75) made with grenadine as the sweetener. Its earliest known appearance was in a 1916 cocktail book simply titled *Drinks*, by Jacques Straub. While it was a very popular cocktail before, during, and after Prohibition, the Bacardí is enjoying something of a renaissance today.

It's interesting to note that in the Bacardí's earlier iterations, there was some variation in its composition. For example, in the fourth edition of *Jack's Manual* (1916) by Jack Grohusko, the Bacardí also included a wee bit of sweet and dry vermouth. And in 1920s Paris, further liberties were taken. Frank Meier at the Paris Ritz added dry vermouth, and at Harry's New York Bar, Harry MacElhone added a bit of gin. Zelda Fitzgerald, who lived in Paris for part of the 1920s, had a special fondness for the Bacardí, which got a mention in her 1929 short story "The Original Follies Girl." In that short story, Zelda described the pro- tagonist: "I saw her not long ago under the trees in the Champs-Élysées. She looked like a daffodil. She was taking a yellow linen sports thing for an airing and she reeked of lemony perfume and Bacardí cocktails." She made her way "up the broad avenue by the mist from the fountains and the glitter of bright flowers in the shadow, the curling blue haze and the smell of excitement that make a Paris summer dusk."

Among many other American expats in 1920s Paris, poet, publisher, and playboy Harry Crosby was also a fan, and you'll find many references to the Bacardí (misspelled "Baccardi") in his diaries, where he tells of attend- ing a "party with the countess Baccardi cocktails champagne," or of drink- ing "Baccardi cocktails with brown sugar," or having a "Baccardi cocktail" at the Ritz bar. Ever the emo poet, in another entry Harry glumly noted that his wife Caresse was leaving Paris on a liner bound for New York, "and it is a gray day and rain is about to fall and it gets dark very early and I drink a rose-gold Baccardi cocktail (always the desire to pray when drinking cocktails)."

Other Bacardí Cocktail devotees included Mary Pickford (see page 142) and Don "Uncle Don" Carney, a vaudeville star. The *Brooklyn Daily Eagle* of March 30, 1934, informed readers that "Mary Pickford and Uncle Don both prefer a Bacardí. Here's the recipe for Mary's: one-half Bacardí rum; one-half pineapple juice; one teaspoon grenadine and six drops maraschino. Uncle Don likes his made with equal parts pineapple and grapefruit juice, a jigger of Bacardí, and a dash of absinthe or anisette." Hmmm, I wonder where the lime juice went? Today, however, the recipe is fairly standard.

makes 1 cocktail

2 ounces Bacardí Superior light rum

3½ ounces grenadine

½ ounce fresh lime juice

Combine all the ingredients in a cocktail shaker filled with ice. Shake well and strain into a chilled cocktail glass.

variation: Add egg white to the Bacardí Cocktail, and you've got a Fireman's Sour, which was popular in the 1930s. Follow the same process, but dry shake (see page 4) before adding ice to the shaker, then shake again.

BAHAMA MAMA

This drink was likely named for a popular Bahamian novelty song from 1932 by Wolfe Gilbert and Charles Lofthouse, which was commonly played for tourists as they arrived in Nassau from the 1930s through the 1960s. An item in the *Philadelphia Inquirer* of May 11, 1947, told of a typical tourist encounter, where "a native boy dressed in pink cotton slacks and a faded blue shirt strums a ukulele and serenades you with 'Bahama Mama' or 'Mama Don' Wan' No Peas, No Rice, No Coconut Oil.'"

We see the first signs of the drink in 1960. The *Fort Lauderdale News* reported on October 4 of that year that "elsewhere, in the mammoth British Colonial [Hotel] Leonce Picot tossed a rum-o-rama party for island dignitaries and the guests of the hotel. The 'Bahama Mama' special concoction for the Nassau-based Gill hotel, was debuted." "Rum-o-rama party?" What's that about?

This "rum-o-rama" gimmick was a program of the Gill Hotels chain, by which a "new collection of custom-concocted tropical drinks" was created, with "a special and different drink for each hotel." Under this promotion, guests at a Gill hotel would receive a "Gill Passport," and each time they'd stay at a given property, they'd be given that hotel's house drink and have their passport stamped. A gossip column called "The Night Watch" by Dick Hoekstra in the *Fort Lauderdale News* of September 27, 1960, explained that "the Escape Hotel would feature a Banana Daiquiri, the Jolly Roger a Salute, the Trade Winds a Sundowner, the Hillsboro a Floridita Daiquiri [see page 75], and the British Colonial in Nassau a Bahama Mama." The article further snarked that "the Yankee Clipper Hotel kicked off the introduction parties with their 'El Morro,'" and that "Manager Tom Brown, through heavy eyelids, explained that this one contains three ounces of Don Q rum alone." Jeez, tough crowd! (Later in that same piece there was mention of a recent performance given by the Ike Cole Trio; Ike was Nat King Cole's brother. It seems Dick Hoekstra was "but mildly impressed. Ike is billed as, and looks like, a younger, fatter facsimile of the famed Nat." Yeesh.)

Anyway, the drink caught on, and by 1961 the Bahama Mama had made it across the continent to the Beverly Hills outpost of Trader Vic's. But like so many tiki and other tropical-themed drinks, it's difficult to pin down the Bahama Mama to one specific recipe; indeed, the Trader Vic's offering might have been a different drink, with coincidentally the same name.

For the definitive recipe, I turned to the *Oxford Companion to Spirits and Cocktails* entry on the Bahama Mama, written by my friend Martin Cate, author of *Smuggler's Cove: Exotic Cocktails, Rum, and the Cult of Tiki.*

makes 1 cocktail

½ ounce dark rum

½ ounce coconut liqueur

¼ ounce coffee liqueur

½ ounce fresh lemon juice

4 ounces pineapple juice

¼ ounce 151-proof rum, to float

1 cocktail cherry, for garnish

Combine the dark rum, coconut liqueur, coffee liqueur, lemon juice, and pineapple juice in a cocktail shaker filled with ice. Shake well, then strain into a chilled cocktail glass. Carefully float (see page 5) the 151 rum atop the drink and garnish with the cocktail cherry.

BEE'S KNEES

The decade known as the Roaring Twenties was a time of many things, both good and bad. We had Prohibition, and a whole class of otherwise law-abiding people who decided to become "Scofflaws" (page 196). We had jazz music, and dances like the Charleston being performed by flappers and their zoot-suit-wearing boyfriends. And we had all kinds of new terms being bandied about, from "twenty-three skiddoo" to "she's the cat's pajamas" to "daddio" and "you're all wet." And one of those wacky phrases was given to a drink: Back in the 1920s, if you thought that the girl you were seeing was just swell, you might find yourself referring to her as "the bee's knees!"

During this era, at the Paris Ritz worked a world-class bartender by the name of Frank Meier. At some point in the 1920s, Frank created a classic sour and gave it the name the "Bee's Knees." As a punctuation aside, note that in Frank's 1936 book, *The Artistry of Mixing Drinks*, he placed the apostrophe *after* the end of the word, not before the letter *s*. As such, ol' Frank must have been referring to the knees of multiple bees, collectively, and not the knees of a particular bee. Hey, how about that?

The Bee's Knees was an early (if not the first) instance of using honey as the sweetener. Get it? Bees? Honey? In my view, the Bee's Knees, along with the Southside (page 204), are drinks that should be served to friends who claim, "Oh, I can't drink gin, I can't stand gin, that one night in college . . ." This drink will change their minds. Trust me.

2 ounces London dry gin

½ ounce fresh lemon juice

½ ounce honey or honey syrup (see page 7)

Combine all the ingredients in a cocktail shaker filled with ice. Shake well and strain into a chilled cocktail glass.

variations: Use bourbon instead of gin and serve it on the rocks in an Old-Fashioned glass and you're drinking a Gold Rush, invented at Milk & Honey in New York circa 2000. The amazing thing about this drink is that it was basically invented by a customer. T. J. Siegal, a friend and business partner of the late, lamented owner, Sasha Petraske, dreamed it up while sitting at the bar! It's become a modern classic; in fact, it inspired the Penicillin (page 174), another modern classic. Speaking of Petraske, also try a drink he called The Business, which is a Bee's Knees made with lime juice in place of the lemon. If you say "Business" and "Bee's Knees" one word after the other you'll see where he got the name (and the inspiration)!

FRANK MEIER

Frank Meier was one of the great bartenders of the twentieth century. Lucius Beebe, in his 1946 *The Stork Club Bar Book*, offered that "Frank of the Ritz Bar was a sort of universally recognized king of saloonkeepers and was, in fact, a very pleasant, generous, and understanding friend to thousands of Americans." In Basil Woon's 1926 guidebook, *The Paris That's Not in the Guidebooks*, he referred to Meier as "possibly the best-known drink shaker in the world, not excluding the individual who does it at the Savoy in London," referring of course to Harry Craddock, head bartender at the Savoy's American Bar. Coincidentally, both Craddock and Meier worked previously at the famed Hoffman House in Manhattan prior to Prohibition.

Woon further noted that "Frank is the most feared man in Parisian society" because of the secrets he held. Bruce Reynolds, in *Paris with the Lid Lifted* (1927) agreed, holding that

> Frank, manager of this astounding shrine . . . can socially make or break a visitor, depending upon the degree of the cordiality of his greeting. To be addressed by Frank, by name, is no mean compliment. And he is the intimate of the scions of great families of America. Millionaires make Frank their confidant and give him tips on the stock market. He knows the business connections, the social connections of all.

Frank would use such social and networking skills for a greater cause during World War II. It's believed that he organized an intelligence ring at the Ritz in support of the French Resistance, and against the Nazi occupiers. Frank's wife was Jewish, so there's no question about his allegiances or motivations.

In *The Artistry of Mixing Drinks,* Frank summed up a key part of his philosophy as follows:

> To know how to drink is as essential as to know how to swim, and one should be at home in both these closely related elements. Each man reacts differently to alcohol; he should know before the time when, according to custom, he indulges in his first collegiate "binge," whether liquor affects his head, his legs, or his morals; whether he sings, fights, weeps, climbs lamp posts, or behaves with excessive affection toward the opposite sex; whether, in short, it makes him a jovial companion or a social pest. A knowledge of these weaknesses will help to overcome them. "Know your capacity and stay within limits." One can drink sensibly, if one knows what a chaos a mixture of liquors can produce. "In vino veritas," so often quoted, does not mean that a man will tell the truth when in drink, but will reveal the hidden side of his character.

BILLIONAIRE
(AND MILLIONAIRE!)

The Billionaire is one of the great creations to come from the bartending duo of Jason Kosmas and Dushan Zaric when they worked at Employees Only in New York City. They invented it while perusing old cocktail books, looking for ideas. They talked about it within the pages of their excellent 2010 book *Speakeasy: The Employees Only Guide to Classic Cocktails Reimagined*:

> This cocktail was created in flash of inspiration to showcase over-proof whiskey by offsetting it with wonderfully lush and flavorful ingredients. Strong Baker's 107-proof bourbon serves as the backbone to the cocktail, providing vigor and heat. This is balanced with our rich homemade grenadine and fresh lemon juice to give a delightful sweet-and-sour balance. The addition of the absinthe bitters' anise essence rounds out the cocktail, giving it a classic feel and third dimension. After conceiving the recipe, we were stumped for a name until we realized it was quite similar to a version of the Prohibition classic Millionaire Cocktail. Because of inflation and the fact that ours is a "richer" cocktail, we named it the Billionaire Cocktail.

Harry Craddock's *The Savoy Cocktail Book* (1930) includes a drink called the Millionaire Cocktail No. 1 (recipe follows). Jason and Dushan were joking around, recalling the famous scene from *Austin Powers, International Man of Mystery* where Dr. Evil, who's been cryogenically frozen for some years, is unaware that holding the entire world hostage for . . . one *miiiiiiillion dollars* was not such a princely sum in 1997! So, presumably with pinkies touching their lips, they both decided that their invention should be named after a more impressive tax bracket.

BILLIONAIRE

makes 1 cocktail

2 ounces Baker's 107-proof bourbon
  (or any good cask-strength bourbon)

1 ounce fresh lemon juice

½ ounce simple syrup (see page 6)

½ ounce Homemade Grenadine (recipe follows)

¼ ounce Absinthe Bitters (recipe follows)

1 lemon wheel, for garnish

Combine the bourbon, lemon juice, simple syrup, grenadine, and bitters in a cocktail shaker filled with ice and shake well. Strain into a chilled cocktail glass and garnish with the lemon wheel.

HOMEMADE GRENADINE

makes about 4 cups

1 cup simple syrup (see page 6)

2½ cups pomegranate juice

½ cup Cardenal Mendoza brandy (or any dark, rich brandy)

In a small saucepan, combine the simple syrup and pomegranate juice and bring to a boil over medium heat. Reduce the heat to maintain a simmer and cook, stirring, until the mixture becomes syrupy. Remove from the heat and let cool, then stir in the brandy. Store in a clean bottle or food-safe container in the refrigerator for up to 2 weeks.

ABSINTHE BITTERS

3 cups Pernod 68 absinthe

½ cup green Chartreuse

1 teaspoon Peychaud's bitters

1 teaspoon Angostura bitters

2 tablespoons Fee Brothers mint bitters

Combine all the ingredients in a clean bottle, ideally with a dasher top. The bitters will keep indefinitely.

---

note: The possibility of a scarcity of Chartreuse (as well as a list of available substitutes) is discussed on page 125.

MILLIONAIRE COCKTAIL NO. 1

makes 1 cocktail

¾ ounce sloe gin (such as Fords or Plymouth)

¾ ounce apricot brandy (such as Blume Marillen apricot eau-de-vie), or
¼ ounce apricot liqueur (such as Rothman & Winter orchard apricot liqueur; see Note)

¾ ounce Jamaican dark rum (such as Appleton or Smith & Cross)

1 ounce fresh lime juice

1 dash grenadine

Combine all the ingredients in a cocktail shaker filled with ice. Shake well and strain into a chilled cocktail glass.

---

note: Similar to making the Delicious Sour (page 79), you need to be careful when following a vintage recipe that calls for a fruit "brandy," because today's offerings are likely to be far sweeter than fruit brandies back in the day. If you cannot find a true (unsweetened) eau-de-vie, use a liqueur; just reduce the amount, since it will otherwise overwhelm the flavor and make the drink too sweet.

BLOOMFIELD

A lovely variation on the Aviation (page 36), this drink was invented in 2020 by Hanna Madagame, the front of house manager and bar manager at Wren in Sutton's Bay, Michigan. Hanna is a big fan of the Aviation, and in her variation, she amps up the drink's distinctive purple color by adding an ingredient she'd seen used by other bartenders at that time: butterfly pea flower powder. Hanna tells me, "The pea powder is pH reactive . . . It turns the cocktail a really rich purple color."

As an aside, my lovely bride enjoys telling Hanna (in my presence, of course) that Hanna makes the best Old-Fashioned she's ever had. This only bothers me a little bit, mainly because it's true.

makes 1 cocktail

2 ounces botanical gin of choice (Hanna uses Grand Traverse Distillery Barrel-Finished Peninsula Gin)

¾ ounce fresh lime juice

½ ounce fresh grapefruit juice

¾ ounce honey syrup (see page 7)

¼ ounce crème de violette

1 teaspoon butterfly pea flower powder (such as Sou Zen 100% pure butterfly pea flower powder)

1 lime wheel, for garnish

Combine the gin, lime juice, grapefruit juice, honey syrup, crème de violette, and butterfly pea flower powder in a cocktail shaker filled with ice and shake well. Strain into a chilled cocktail glass and garnish with the lime wheel.

---

note: For another drink using butterfly pea flower powder, try the Miss Saigon (page 150).

BRAMBLE

The Bramble is a great example of how the Sour cocktail can serve as a canvas for innovation. This drink, after all, is nothing more than a Gin Sour at its core. Let's say you've made that Gin Sour, but you're a bit bored with the result. Add soda water and serve it on ice, and now it's a refreshing Tom Collins (page 214). Or pour it back into the shaker and add mint leaves, shake it well, then strain into a tall glass with ice, top it with soda water, and wham—it's a Southside. Or get a bottle of blackberry liqueur and after pouring the drink, drizzle some of it into your glass, et voilà—you've made a Bramble.

This (somewhat) modern classic was invented by legendary London barman Dick Bradsell (creator of the Espresso Martini) in 1989 while he was behind the stick at Fred's Club in the Soho part of England's capital city. According to my friends Anistatia Miller and Jared Brown, writing on this drink in *The Oxford Companion to Spirits and Cocktails*: "Bradsell based the drink on a version of the Singapore Sling he made previously at the Zanzibar, a private members' club. . . . The drink was intended to be a salute to British flavors . . . the crème de mûre evoked memories for Bradsell of the blackberries that grow on the Isle of Wight."

makes 1 cocktail

2 ounces London dry gin

1 ounce fresh lemon juice

½ ounce rich simple syrup (see page 6), or perhaps less, depending on how sweet you want it (remember, you're adding a sweetish liqueur later!)

½ ounce crème de mûre (blackberry liqueur; Massenez makes a fine version)

1 blackberry, for garnish

1 lemon slice, for garnish

Combine the gin, lemon juice, and simple syrup in a cocktail shaker filled with ice and shake well. Strain into an Old-Fashioned glass filled with crushed ice, then carefully drizzle the crème de mûre on the surface of the drink and admire the way it bleeds down into the cocktail. Garnish with the blackberry and lemon slice.

BROWN DERBY
(HOLLYWOOD-STYLE, AKA THE DE RIGUEUR)

You know the old expression, "That's Hollywood"—meaning that, in a town built on fantasy, storytelling, "Hollywood endings," and impossibly beautiful stars, it's to be expected that what's before your eyes *isn't really real*. Consistent with that theme, here's a "classic cocktail" that's as phony as so many of the other façades of Tinseltown.

The Brown Derby was an iconic chain of restaurants, the first two in the Los Angeles area. The original location, shaped like a brown derby hat, opened on Wilshire Boulevard in 1926, and the Hollywood venue debuted in 1929 on North Vine Street. The latter of the two became the place to be seen and to make deals for those in the movie biz.

Okay, back to that bit about phoniness. See, in 1933 a fellow named George Buzza Jr. published a book titled *Hollywood Cocktails*, which purported to be "Hollywood's Favorite Cocktail Book, including the favorite cocktail served at each of the smartest stars' rendezvous." But according to my friend Greg Boehm, it was all a fraud: "All but eight of the 222 recipes were copied verbatim from *The Savoy Cocktail Book*," and many of those were renamed to correspond to Hollywood names and places. I'm shocked, *shocked* to find there's phoniness going on in Hollywood! But it's still a good drink!

The recipe for this cocktail was a word-for-word rip-off of a drink that had appeared three years earlier in 1930 in Harry Craddock's *The Savoy Cocktail Book* called the De Rigueur. Ironic, eh? That the concept of phoniness, which is de rigueur in Hollywood, would exist even when it comes to "Hollywood cocktails"? But that's Hollywood. Can you imagine the eyerolls from the bartenders at the various joints mentioned in Buzza's book, each time some starry-eyed tourist walked in with their dog-eared copy of that bloody book under their arm? "Can you make me a Brown Derby? I hear it's the house drink here!" Sigh . . . Phoniness aside, let's make that drink.

2 ounces bourbon

1 ounce fresh grapefruit juice

½ ounce honey syrup (see page 7)

Combine all the ingredients in a cocktail shaker filled with ice. Shake well and strain into a chilled cocktail glass.

> **variation:** There was another Brown Derby cocktail, the so-called East Coast rum version, which made no claims to being connected to the Hollywood scene. First mentioned in *Esquire* magazine in 1935, it enjoyed a bit of celebrity on the New York City cocktail circuit in the 1930s, and is made with 2 ounces dark rum, 1 ounce fresh lime juice, and a heaping teaspoon of maple syrup, shaken, strained, and served up. It's basically a dark rum and maple syrup Daiquiri, and it is quite nice.

BRUTE FORCE

Jillian Vose, formerly of the legendary New York bar the Dead Rabbit and now proprietor of Hazel and the Apple, an Irish-themed bar in Charleston, South Carolina, created this drink, a riff on the margarita, for the Dead Rabbit in 2016. "Green tea, absinthe, and pear was the flavor combination I was going for, and with a little bit of flip-flopping and swapping of my sweetener and modifier (I ended up using orgeat instead of the logical agave, and pear liqueur as an obvious substitute for the Cointreau)," she says. The tequila is infused with green tea, and a couple dashes of absinthe accent all the flavors in the drink.

makes 1 cocktail

1½ ounces Green Tea–Infused Blanco Tequila (recipe follows)

¾ ounce fresh lime juice

½ ounce orgeat

½ ounce pear liqueur (such as Mathilde or Rothman & Winter)

¼ ounce Wray & Nephew Overproof White Rum

2 dashes absinthe verte (such as Vieux Pontarlier or Pernod)

Freshly grated nutmeg, for garnish

Combine the infused tequila, lime juice, orgeat, pear liqueur, overproof rum, and absinthe in a cocktail shaker filled with ice and shake well. Strain into an Old-Fashioned glass with one large ice cube and garnish with nutmeg.

GREEN TEA-INFUSED BLANCO TEQUILA

makes 1 liter

1 (1-liter) bottle blanco tequila (Altos Blanco or El Tresoro Blanco)

2 grams loose green tea leaves, or 1 green tea bag

Pour the tequila into an airtight container and stir in the green tea. Let stand for 10 to 15 minutes. Strain through cheesecloth or a coffee filter into the original bottle and discard the tea leaves (or remove and discard the tea bag and pour the tequila into the original bottle). Seal and label the bottle and store at room temperature. It will keep indefinitely.

CAIPIRINHA

The Caipirinha is a drink that's been enjoying a bit of the cocktail renaissance limelight in recent years. A Brazilian import, made with cachaça, muddled lime, and sugar, it made its first appearance in 1970s American newspapers, restaurant reviews, and travel stories. Cachaça is a sugarcane-based spirit from Brazil, made directly from cane juice (and not molasses), similar to rhum agricole (see page 57). For whatever reason, however, we're not supposed to call cachaça "Brazilian rum." The name "Caipirinha" in Brazilian Portuguese means something akin to "country bumpkin" or "hillbilly," as in an unsophisticated rube.

The Caipirinha has become known, at least to the rest of the world, as the national drink of Brazil. Newspapers from March 1978 reported that during an eight-day goodwill visit to that country, England's then-Prince (now King) Charles stopped off in São Paulo, where he was warmly greeted by about two thousand locals: "He chatted with scores of Britons and sampled 'caipirinha' (a sugar-lemon-rum drink). He called it a 'good brew.'"

The drink was just one of a family of Brazilian drinks known as *batidas*, the Caipirinha being known as the Batida Paulista (suggesting that it perhaps originated, or was popular in, São Paulo, Brazil's largest city). According to *The Oxford Companion to Spirits and Cocktails*, a *batida*, as defined in Roberto Costa's 1974 work *Traçado geral das Batidas*, is a "cold aperitive that is essentially made with cachaça, sugar, fruits, juices, or essences and ice, shaken in a cocktail shaker or mixed in a blender." Here's how to make that Caipirinha.

2 ounces cachaça

2 teaspoons sugar

1 lime, cut into wedges

1 lime wheel, for garnish

Muddle the cachaça, sugar, and lime wedges in a sturdy Old-Fashioned glass until the sugar has dissolved and the juice and essence of the lime have been extracted. Add ice and stir well. Garnish with the lime wheel.

variations: During the 1980s, fashionable Brazilians felt that the Caipirinha, like the definition says, was a bit backward or rustic. They began to enjoy a drink made with vodka in place of the cachaça, and they called it the Caipiroska. For a different impression, use a white rum in place of the cachaça for a Caipirissima. And while we're talking about "national drinks," do check out Martinique's: the Ti' Punch (short for "petite punch"). It's similar to the Caipirinha but made with rhum agricole, a lime peel or wedge, and sugar or cane syrup, muddled in the glass with some ice. Rhum agricole, which is the preferred rum of the French Caribbean Islands such as Martinique and Guadeloupe, is distilled from sugarcane juice, not from the molasses left over after sugar is refined (as is the case with most rums), and has a distinctly funky, vegetal aroma and flavor. Meanwhile, don't sleep on Kenya's take on the Caipirinha, known as the Dawa; it's made the same way as the Caipiroska, but with additional sweetening coming from a "dawa stick," a slender rod dipped in honey. Lastly, try the Rio Brava, made with cachaça, lime juice, orgeat, ginger, and orange zest and peel. As the Brazilians would say, *saúde!*

CHARBONNEAU WAY

This drink comes from my friend Abby Gullo, a bartender based in New Orleans by way of both the Beagle and Fort Defiance bars in New York City. This drink, an ode to her upstate New York and French Canadian roots (with an absinthe rinse in honor of her current home), is named for the road up to her family's sugar house in the Catskill Mountains, where they made their own maple syrup. ("I still remember running up and down the hill with buckets of tree sap in the winter and bringing them into the steamy hot sugar house for my aunts and uncles to boil down into syrup.) There was also wild mountain thyme, which they'd use to make maple syrup Juleps in the summer.

This drink, which has been on the menu of all of the bars Abby has worked at for years, is one of my favorite contemporary drinks. I love how the bitterness of the Suze plays against the sweetness of the maple syrup and the sourness of the lemon. I also love the other tidbit of family lore that Abby shared with me: "We have a cousin who was on the Lewis and Clark expedition, Toussaint Charbonneau, but he was kind of a jerk, so we are more proud of his wife, Sacagawea."

makes 1 cocktail

¼ ounce absinthe

2 ounces rye whiskey (Rittenhouse works great, or Willett if you can find it!)

¾ ounce fresh lemon juice

½ ounce pure maple syrup

½ ounce Suze

1 thyme sprig, for garnish

Rinse (see page 5) the inside of a chilled cocktail glass with the absinthe, then set the glass aside. Combine the whiskey, lemon juice, maple syrup, and Suze in a cocktail shaker filled with ice and shake well. Strain into the absinthe-rinsed glass and garnish with the thyme.

CHARLIE CHAPLIN

Named for the legendary British entertainer, the earliest-known reference to this drink was in the 1931 book *Old Waldorf Bar Days* by Albert Stevens Crockett. Written during Prohibition, the book was a nostalgic chronicle of all the great drinks invented or popular at the Waldorf-Astoria Hotel in New York City. It was subtitled *With the Cognomina and Composition of Four Hundred and Ninety-One Appealing Appetizers and Salutary Potations Long Known, Admired and Served at the Famous Big Brass Rail; also, a Glossary for the Use of Antiquarians and Students of American Mores.* Thirsty yet? In one passage of the book, titled "Concerning the Curriculum," the author noted that "Charlie Chaplin had a cocktail named in his honor when he began to make the screen public laugh." Makes sense to me.

Prohibition did eventually end, on December 5, 1933. In rapt anticipation of that momentous date, newspapers building up to what we now know as "Repeal Day" began to whet the appetites of their readers who were primed to wet their whistles. In a full-page story in the November 12, 1933, edition of the *New York Daily News* titled "For Tomorrow We Drink," columnist Anne Fisher breathlessly wrote, "Eat and be merry for tomorrow—or in just a few weeks, anyway—we drink! For that reason, the *News* sent a reporter here and there to this famous bartender and that famous bar, to gather up some of the recipes for the best-known mixed drinks. They are printed herewith, to be read with reverence and be mixed with due ceremony." Let's remember, after nearly fourteen years of Prohibition, during which you would drink whatever you could get your hands on, Americans had to relearn how a proper cocktail was made.

The article offered recipes for a number of classics, including "Several Waldorf Cocktails," notably the Charlie Chaplin. It was described succinctly as being composed of "one-third lime juice, one-third sloe gin, one-third apricot brandy," precisely how it was listed in *Old Waldorf Bar Days*. Cheers to consistency!

recipe continues →

1 ounce sloe gin (such as Fords or Plymouth)

1 ounce fresh lime juice

1 ounce apricot brandy (such as Blume Marillen apricot eau-de-vie), or
¼ ounce apricot liqueur (such as Rothman & Winter orchard apricot
liqueur; see Note)

Combine all the ingredients in a cocktail shaker filled with ice. Shake well and strain into a chilled cocktail glass.

---

note: Similar to making the Delicious Sour (page 79) and the Millionaire (page 48), you need to be careful when following a vintage recipe that calls for a fruit "brandy," because today's offerings are likely going to be far sweeter than the fruit brandies offered back in the day. If you cannot find a true (unsweetened) eau-de-vie, you can use a liqueur; just reduce the amount used, since it will otherwise overwhelm the flavor and make the drink too sweet.

---

variation: My good friend Frank Caiafa, who ran the bar at both the Peacock Alley and La Chine restaurants of the Waldorf-Astoria from 2005 until the hotel's closure in 2017, published an updated version of *The Waldorf Astoria Bar Book* in 2016. In that book, he reimagined the Charlie Chaplin to include 1 ounce of London dry gin with the original formula. In my opinion, this makes it a superior drink, with the gin adding backbone and drying it out a bit.

CHARTREUSE SWIZZLE

Invented by my friend Marco Dionysos at Tres Agaves in San Francisco, circa 2002, this drink certainly qualifies as a modern classic. It marries two flavors that were born to go together—green Chartreuse and pineapple—with lime juice for tartness and falernum for sweetness and a silky mouthfeel. To me, green Chartreuse's herbal oomph has always been something of an acquired taste, and so the pineapple tends to soften its edges a bit and makes it a lot more accessible. Call it a gateway drink for appreciating Chartreuse. It's a delicious summertime cooler, and you don't even need to use a swizzle stick!

makes 1 cocktail

1½ ounces green Chartreuse

1 ounce pineapple juice

¾ ounce fresh lime juice

½ ounce falernum

1 pineapple wedge and/or mint sprig, for garnish

Combine the Chartreuse, pineapple juice, lime juice, and falernum in a cocktail shaker filled with ice and shake well. Strain into a Collins glass filled with crushed ice and garnish with the pineapple wedge and/or mint sprig.

> *note:* The possibility of a scarcity of Chartreuse, as well as range of available substitutes, is discussed on page 125.

CHURCHILL

I can't think of an historic establishment that sports a more illustrious roster of bartenders than the American Bar at the Savoy Hotel in London. Since its opening in 1893, its staff has included the likes of Ruth "Kitty" Burgess, Ada "Coley" Coleman, Harry Craddock, Eddie Clark, J. Reginald "Johnnie" Johnson, Peter Dorelli, Erik Lorincz, and more recently Shannon Tebay (the first American to serve as head bartender) and Chelsie Bailey. For most of the twentieth century, the Savoy served as the *ne plus ultra* in terms of the quality of its food and drink.

During the middle portion of this great hotel's history, Joe Gilmore presided over the American Bar from 1954 to 1975. He would provide his inimitable style of hospitality to many of the world's great celebrities, including former Prime Minister Winston Churchill (1874–1965).

Churchill was quite fond of bending the old elbow, and if there was ever a highly functioning drinker, it was he. He had a saying: "When I was younger, I made it a rule never to take strong drink before lunch. It is now my rule never to do so before breakfast." But that never seemed to slow him down at all. As Antoine Capet related in his entry in *Alcohol and Temperance in Modern History*, Churchill once boasted that "I've taken more out of alcohol than it has taken out of me." His daily schedule, including those epic days as British prime minister, when it appeared he was singlehandedly saving democracy from the Nazis, included wine at breakfast; Port, Champagne, or brandy at meals, and wee drams of whisky throughout the day. But it seemed "that he had a super-human capacity for absorbing hard liquor without getting intoxicated. Aides and foreign statesmen have remarked in their war memoirs how he could conduct the most momentous discussions on complicated strategic decisions in perfect lucidity after imbibing a quantity of drink that would have made most mortals lose their consciousness."

In most ways, Churchill was the quintessential Englishman except, however, when it came to England's drink of choice, tea. According to historian Robert Rhodes James, during a gathering in the Smoking Room of the House of Commons, when a young Conservative member of Parliament asked if

Churchill would care for a spot of tea, Churchill blasted his kind offer: "Don't be a bloody fool. I want a *large* glass of whisky." It seems he developed a taste for the stuff while serving in the British military in 1897 in India and never looked back. After all, the water in India was undrinkable, unless you cut it with either lime juice or whisky.

Which brings us back to the Savoy. During Joe Gilmore's reign as head bartender, he developed a drink, presumably with the cooperation of one of his favorite clients, Mr. Churchill, who would lend his name to the finished product. Perhaps the idea of lime juice and whisky took Winnie back to his salad days in India, when he was just a young man serving the Crown, trying to avoid, you know, *drinking tea.*

makes 1 cocktail

1½ ounces Scotch

½ ounce Cointreau

½ ounce sweet vermouth

½ ounce fresh lime juice

Combine all the ingredients in a cocktail shaker filled with ice. Shake well and strain into a chilled cocktail glass.

CLOVER CLUB

This is a cocktail that had quite a moment from the time of its invention (around 1900) until Prohibition, at which time it slipped into obscurity, only to have been revived in recent years. It was the house drink at an exclusive men's club in Philadelphia of the same name. The Club existed from 1882 until 1914, holding monthly dinners at the Bellevue-Stratford Hotel in Center City, Philadelphia. Newspapers in May 1909 spoke of the drink as "appropriate for warm days," and that it "is mild and refreshing." So proud of its "local boy made good," the *Philadelphia Inquirer* of April 10, 1910, bragged that "The 'Clover Club cocktail' is fast becoming the rage in New York. All of the actors drink it now and the bartenders of the Plaza can teach the man who invented them the art of mixing." And, according to a January 22, 1913, item in the *Brooklyn Times Union*, president William Howard Taft paid a visit to the Club itself. Ever the politician, President Taft quipped that "no national administration is complete until its President had received his baptism in the Clover Club." To which the *Times Union* retorted, "With the Clover Club cocktail as the baptismal font?"

The Clover Club even had its own drinking toast, found within the pages of Paul E. Lowe's 1904 book *Drinks as They Are Mixed*:

> Here's to a long life and a merry one,
> A quick death and a happy one,
> A good girl and a pretty one,
> A cold bottle and another one.

But back to that drink. As America emerged from Prohibition and was raring to get back into the drinking habit, it had lost its pre-dry-times sweet tooth. As a result, the Clover Club fell out of favor, so much so that in 1934, *Esquire* magazine named it among its "Ten Worst Cocktails." The drink remained hidden in the dusty cocktail books of yore until world-renowned bartender (and friend) Julie Reiner opened her bar of the same name in Brooklyn circa 2008, with a revised version of the Clover Club cocktail as its house drink.

Revised how? Julie took a page from a 1909 cocktail book that had a slightly different recipe for the drink. The original recipe called for 2 ounces of Plymouth gin, ½ ounce of fresh lemon juice, about ⅓ ounce of raspberry syrup, and 1 egg white, all of which were shaken well with ice and strained into a chilled cocktail glass. The 1909 version, from Paul E. Lowe's book *Drinks: How to Mix and How to Serve*, went something like this:

makes 1 cocktail

1 ounce Plymouth gin

½ ounce dry vermouth

½ ounce fresh lemon juice

⅓ ounce raspberry syrup

1 medium egg white

1 mint leaf, for garnish

Combine the gin, vermouth, lemon juice, raspberry syrup, and egg white in a shaker without ice and do a dry shake (see page 4), then add ice and shake well again. Strain into a chilled cocktail glass and garnish with the mint leaf.

variation: To make a Clover Leaf, first either muddle 4 mint leaves in the shaker, then follow the directions for the Clover Club, or shake them in the shaker with the rest of the Clover Club ingredients; either way, garnish with a mint leaf atop the drink. This drink was on the menu of what's purported to be the world's first "Sunday noon cocktail party," held at the home of St. Louis socialite Mrs. Julius S. Walsh in March 1917.

COLOR OF LAW

This little gem was created by Deke Dunn, bar director and one of the creative geniuses at Allegory at the Eaton Hotel in Washington, DC.

Having visited Allegory many times, I can tell you that its artistic theme is really cool. It reimagines Lewis Carroll's *Alice's Adventures in Wonderland*, but depicted through the lens of Ruby Bridges, who was the first Black child to integrate the William Frantz Elementary School in Louisiana in 1960. Consistent with that theme, Deke named this drink after the *New York Times* bestseller *The Color of Law: A Forgotten History of How Our Government Segregated America* by Richard Rothstein. The book chronicles the very intentional ways in which economic opportunity (largely through home ownership) was stymied by federal, state, and local government in the post–World War II years and beyond.

As for the actual drink, Deke tells me that he "was inspired to make this cocktail because I wanted to highlight all the flavors of an India pale ale (IPA) in cocktail form. I don't like IPAs; however, I do appreciate their flavors and complexity, namely, the tropical, citrus, and bitter notes. I wanted to showcase those flavors and complexity in a cocktail. The cocktail came out a pale color, which also helped to inspire the name."

makes 1 cocktail

¾ ounce Hops-Infused Bourbon (recipe follows)

¾ ounce Armagnac

½ ounce Martini & Rossi Ambrato vermouth

5 ounces Fassionola Syrup (recipe follows)

¼ ounce honey syrup (see page 7)

¾ ounce fresh lemon juice

¼ ounce fresh red grapefruit juice

1 grapefruit slice, for garnish

Combine the infused bourbon, Armagnac, vermouth, fassionola syrup, honey syrup, lemon juice, and grapefruit juice in a cocktail shaker filled with ice and shake well. Strain into a chilled cocktail glass and garnish with the grapefruit slice.

HOPS-INFUSED BOURBON

makes about 5 ounces

5 ounces bourbon

1 tablespoon hops (such as cascade)

Combine the bourbon and hops in a container and let stand for 30 minutes. Strain through a fine-mesh sieve into a clean airtight container, cover, and label. It should keep indefinitely.

FASSIONOLA SYRUP

makes 6½ ounces

5 ounces simple syrup (see page 6)

½ ounce pineapple chunks

½ ounce mango chunks

½ ounce passion fruit puree

Combine all the ingredients in a blender and blend until smooth and well combined. Strain through a fine-mesh sieve into an airtight bottle or container and cover. Label and store in the refrigerator for 3 to 4 weeks.

CORPSE REVIVER NO. 2

Here's a curious story: Back at the turn of the last century and into the twentieth century, "American-style" bars in London were fond of making all varieties of drinks in the American style. At this time, the cocktail was one of the United States's greatest cultural exports, so it followed that bartenders could make you a Manhattan, Martini, Knickerbocker, Mint Julep, Sherry Cobbler, or whatever you were used to drinking stateside. But among these "American cocktails" was a class of drinks that, in the words of *The Oxford Companion to Spirits and Cocktails*, "was unknown in America." Wait, what? Indeed, there arose a category of drinks known as "Corpse Revivers" that were intended to offer the customer that extra kick to help them get past their overindulgence from the night before: you know, the proverbial "hair of the dog." Ironically, they were touted as "American cocktails," yet they weren't.

A Corpse Reviver with no numerical designation could be found in the 1937 *Café Royal Cocktail Book* (by William Tarling of the United Kingdom Bartenders' Guild). It was made with equal parts brandy, orange juice, and lemon juice and two dashes of grenadine that was shaken, strained, topped with Champagne—and there you go, Bob's your uncle. Also in the *Café Royal* book was Godfrey's Corpse Reviver (invented by Godfrey Baldini), featuring two parts gin, one part vodka, and a dash each of grenadine and Angostura—shake, strain, cheerio, gov'na!—as well as what they called the New Corpse Reviver, which sounded like the previously referenced No. 1. Then there was a Corpse Reviver No. 1 from Harry Craddock's 1930 *The Savoy Cocktail Book*, which was more of a Manhattan variation, featuring brandy, Calvados, and sweet vermouth. Contemporary bartenders have created their own new riffs on this class, such as the No. 4, among others.

The one version that seems to have stuck is the Corpse Reviver No. 2, and we can thank my dear friend Ted "Dr. Cocktail" Haigh, who included it in his essential book, *Vintage Spirits and Forgotten Cocktails*, for that.

One final point: In *The Savoy Cocktail Book,* Harry Craddock made the cheeky observation that "four of these taken in swift succession will unrevive the corpse again." Ted Haigh also cautioned that "this is one of those cocktails that must be exactly measured to perform its magic." I strongly encourage you to heed both bits of wisdom!

makes 1 cocktail

1 ounce London dry gin

1 ounce Cointreau

1 ounce Lillet Blanc or Cocchi Americano

1 ounce fresh lemon juice

1 to 3 drops absinthe (or another anise or pastis, such as Pernod, Herbsaint, or Ricard, but use sparingly!)

1 cocktail cherry, for garnish

Combine the gin, Cointreau, Lillet Blanc, lemon juice, and absinthe in a cocktail shaker filled with ice and shake well. Strain into a chilled cocktail glass. Garnish with the cocktail cherry, letting it sink to the bottom of the glass.

variations: To stay with the drink's nominally morbid theme, if you want to try something to honor Mexico's Día de los Muertos (Day of the Dead), try the Mezcal Corpse Reviver (Cocchi Americano, mezcal, absinthe, orange curaçao, lime juice, and grapefruit juice). But if you're more into the whole "I'm not dead yet!" theme, try the Twentieth Century (London dry gin, Lillet Blanc, crème de cacao, lemon juice).

COSMOPOLITAN

"Yes, I'd like a cheeseburger, please, large fries, and a Cosmopolitan?" says Carrie Bradshaw, played by Sarah Jessica Parker, placing a McDonald's drive-through order. Sort of.

If someone were to ask you, "Hey, we're having a *Sex and the City* watch party this Friday night, what drink should we serve?" then I think the answer would probably be pretty easy. When the series became a feature film in 2008, the Cosmo had a cameo: Miranda (Cynthia Nixon) and Carrie (Sarah Jessica Parker) are in a swanky cocktail bar (of course) having a Cosmo (of course), and Miranda asks, "Why did we ever stop drinking these?" Carrie's reply? "Because everyone else started."

But it wasn't *Sex and the City* that launched the Cosmo into the popular conscience. That likely happened two years before the series debuted, when Madonna was photographed having one at the Rainbow Room, made for her by Dale DeGroff. When people saw her holding that gorgeous pink drink in a stemmed Martini glass, the question went from "Who's that girl?" to "What's that drink?" And even though the term didn't exist at the time, the photo "went viral," and so did the drink. It became the iconic cocktail of the 1990s, and a big part of the cocktail renaissance we continue to enjoy today.

2 ounces Absolut Citron vodka

1 ounce fresh lime juice

1 ounce Cointreau

1 ounce cranberry juice

1 lime wheel, for garnish

Combine the vodka, lime juice, Cointreau, and cranberry juice in a cocktail shaker filled with ice. Shake well and strain into a chilled cocktail glass. Garnish with a lime wheel.

variations: Believe it or not, the oh-so-sophisticated Cosmopolitan could be said to have descended from the lowly Kamikaze shot, all the rage in the meat market bars of the 1980s, which is made with equal parts vodka, orange curaçao, and lime juice (or, more likely, lime juice cordial). All it's missing is the cranberry! To make the Kamikaze more like a balanced sour, you can increase the vodka to about 2 ounces and use ½ ounce of the other two ingredients, shake, and strain. (With respect to the ratio, as Robert Simonson stated in *The Oxford Companion to Spirits and Cocktails*, "Delicacy of execution was never the hallmark of this drink.") One other drink from cheesy bars in the 1970s and '80s deserves mention here—the Lemon Drop: 2 ounces vodka, 1 ounce simple syrup, 1 ounce (or more) lemon juice. One last variation: Use pomegranate juice in place of the cranberry and lemon juice instead of lime, and you've made a Pomegranate Martini.

CUZCO COCKTAIL

This dangerously refreshing drink is yet another delicious cocktail to make with pisco, the unaged brandy from Peru (see also the Pisco Sour, page 182; and the Pisco Punch, page 179). I found this drink within the pages of Gary Regan's revised and updated *The Joy of Mixology*. Gary tells us that it was adapted from a recipe by Julie Reiner (see page 65), inspired by a trip to Peru that included Regan and "a bunch of other mixologists."

Regan also wrote about the drink in the *San Francisco Chronicle*, noting that the first time Regan made the drink using Reiner's recipe, she stuck her finger into the drink, then flicked a few drops of it onto the barroom floor, as an offering to "Pachamama." When Regan asked who this Pachamama person was, she explained, "Pachamama is Mother Earth, and some Peruvians give Her a few drops of the fruits of Her loins before taking a drink for themselves. It's an old Incan custom that I've sort of adopted."

makes 1 cocktail

½ ounce kirschwasser

2 ounces pisco

¾ ounce Aperol

½ ounce fresh lemon juice

½ ounce fresh grapefruit juice

¾ ounce simple syrup (see page 6)

1 grapefruit peel

Rinse (see page 5) a highball glass with the kirschwasser, fill it with ice, then set it aside. Combine the pisco, Aperol, lemon juice, grapefruit juice, and simple syrup in a cocktail shaker filled with ice and shake well. Strain into the rinsed glass, express the oils from the grapefruit peel over the drink, then use the peel as a garnish.

DADE CITY SOUR

This excellent drink was offered to me by Nick Crutchfield, director of advocacy and education at Lyre's Non-Alcoholic Spirits. (He's also responsible for one of my more fun moments as an author: In 2013, he invited me to guest bartend during Charlotteville, VA's annual Festival of the Book. One of my customers that day was none other Maria Rodriguez, who played the character Maria on *Sesame Street*. It was an honor to fix her a drink, and she also bought a copy of one of my books. All of this enhanced my credibility with my three daughters.) The drink is named after the biggest kumquat festival in the US, held annually in Dade City, Florida, where Nick often visited with his aunt Elsie, creating fond memories of feasting on all things tart and citric. Later, while living in San Diego, which thrives on year-round citrus, he became a regular at a local farmers' market, where he'd buy pints of kumquats weekly. He and his partner, Stacey, would pickle them, candy them, and make salad dressings from the little tart citric bombs. The recipe has evolved over the years; for example, he originally used Hayman's Navy Strength Gin, but he uses Roku, which showcases the drink's adaptability. And as Nick is now working with Lyre's, a premier brand of nonalcoholic spirits, he's also offered a nonalcoholic version of this drink within this recipe.

recipe continues →

1½ ounces Roku Gin (or Lyre's Pink London Spirit for a nonalcoholic version)

¾ ounce fresh lemon juice

1 tablespoon St. Dalfour kumquat preserves (or any good marmalade)

¼ ounce aquafaba (see page 10)

1 spritz of yuzu bitters from an atomizer (or just a dash if you don't have an atomizer; Nick recommends Miracle Mile or the Japanese Bitters Company)

3 slices fresh kumquat or orange peels, for garnish

Combine the gin, lemon juice, preserves, and aquafaba in a cocktail shaker filled with ice and shake well. Strain into a chilled cocktail glass, spray or dash the bitters atop the surface of the drink, then gently rest the kumquat slices or orange peels atop the foam of the drink as a garnish.

DAIQUIRI

"We stayed up late and I drank a few highly frozen Daiquiris just to see what their effect would be (it was moderately terrific and made me feel a friend of all mankind)." This is from a letter Ernest Hemingway wrote to his eleven-year-old son Patrick in 1939.

The Daiquiri is one of the all-time classic cocktails. It's survived the terrible frozen slushie drink fad of the 1970s through . . . well, I guess it hasn't ended yet, as you can *still* get some pretty badly made drinks here and there. No, the Daiquiri has endured, and is and has always been a darling of popular culture.

The drink is believed to have been "invented" by an American mining engineer, Jennings Cox, around the turn of the last century in the little village of Daiquiri, Cuba, just a few miles east of Santiago. As the story goes, he was getting ready to entertain some visiting friends and discovered, to his horror, that he was out of gin (!). He quickly assessed what he had on hand (rum, limes, sugar, ice) and whipped up a batch of drinks, and christened them after the name of his village. A few years later, during a stop on the worldwide tour of the so-called Great White Fleet of US battleships, the USS *Minnesota* paid a visit to Santiago. The skipper and his chief medical officer, Lucius Johnson, somehow met up with Cox. He invited them over for drinks, and Johnson was so impressed with Cox's invention that he brought it back to the States with him. As the story continues, Johnson told folks at the Army and Navy Club in Washington, DC, about the drink, and it became a fixture there, as well as the favorite drink of the Kennedy White House. The Daiquiri had been launched. (If you're wondering why I used quotes when I said the Daiquiri was "invented" by Jennings Cox, in my mind the three-part platform that makes up the Daiquiri was known to folks in Cuba long before Americans showed up to figure it out.)

But while the Daiquiri was born in southeast Cuba and launched in DC, it flourished in Havana. There, in a bar/restaurant called La Florida, which went by the diminutive El Floridita, bartender/owner Constantino "Constante" Ribalaigua Vert embraced the drink and became its master. Over the course of the 1930s, he'd develop at least six variations on the Daiquiri, and he was one of the first, if not the first, to use the recently invented Waring blender to make frozen Daiquiris. Indeed, Constante built the reputation of El Floridita as being "the Cradle of the Daiquiri."

Constante's Daiquiri No. 1 was the classic, with light rum, lime juice, sugar, cracked ice, shaken and strained. No. 2 was the No. 1 but with "several dashes" orange curaçao and a teaspoon of orange juice. No. 3 was just the No. 1 but with a teaspoon each of grapefruit juice and maraschino liqueur. No. 4 was the No. 3, sans grapefruit juice. No. 5 was the No. 4 but with the addition of a teaspoon of grenadine (they referred to it as the Pink Daiquiri).

Then you had the (misspelled) "E. Henmiway Special," named after one of the bar's regulars, Ernest Hemingway. In the 1937 edition of El Floridita's cocktail menu, which mangled the spelling of Hemingway's name, this drink was basically the No. 3, but without sugar, since Hemingway was concerned about diabetes. Hemingway had been coming to Havana from Key West, both to fish and write, since March 1929, often accompanied by his good friend and fishing buddy Joe Russell, owner of Sloppy Joe's in Key West. During one of those visits he discovered El Floridita and, of course, the Daiquiri. Hemingway would eventually ask the bartenders to make him a double-sized drink, which came to be known as the Papa Doble. It became one of Hemingway's favorite drinks while living in Cuba, and he spent countless hours at the far-left end of the bar drinking Daiquiris. Nowadays, the end of that bar favored by Papa is marked by a life-size bronze statue of Hemingway, waiting for his next Daiquiri. You'll find it in Hemingway's *Islands in the Stream* (such as in an autobiographical scene in which the Papa-esque protagonist sets the house record at Havana's El Floridita bar, drinking seventeen frozen Daiquiris!).

Lauren Bacall's character Slim sips one in the 1944 film *To Have and Have Not* (when she was only nineteen!), and it's in Tennessee Williams's one-act play *Suddenly Last Summer* (featuring the eccentric Violet Venable, living in New Orleans's Garden District, who insisted on having a frozen Daiquiri every day at five o'clock: "You could set a watch by it!"). That doesn't sound eccentric to me, just sayin.' And speaking of New Orleans, they *still* have drive-through Daiquiri bars down there. Now *that's* eccentric. Here's how to make that Daiquiri.

2 ounces light rum

¾ ounce fresh lime juice

½ teaspoon sugar, or ½ ounce simple syrup (see page 6)

1 lime wheel, for garnish

Combine the rum, lime juice, and sugar in a cocktail shaker filled with ice and shake well. Strain into a chilled cocktail glass and garnish with the lime wheel.

variations: Use honey syrup (see page 7) in place of the sugar or simple syrup, and you've got a Honeysuckle Daiquiri (see also the similarly named Margarita variation using honey syrup on page 141). Or add a grapefruit peel to the shaker and give it a good shake, and you've made a Regal Daiquiri, invented circa 2010 by Theo Lieberman at Milk & Honey and/or Lantern's Keep in New York City. Or try the Hollywood Avenue Cocktail, made with aged rum, lemon juice, grapefruit juice, honey syrup, Angostura bitters, and, believe it or not, Dijon mustard. It's surprisingly good!

To make a Hemingway Daiquiri, shake 2 ounces light rum, ½ ounce fresh lime juice, ⅓ ounce grapefruit juice, and 1 teaspoon maraschino liqueur and strain into a chilled cocktail glass. Or, of course, you can blend it à la Constante Ribalaigua. Meanwhile, I've invented the Statin Islander, a grapefruit-free version for those who are on statin drugs and should avoid grapefruit; it replaces the grapefruit juice with ½ ounce Campari and ¼ ounce Cointreau.

recipe continues →

For another variation, try the one invented by writer Edgar Rice Burroughs, creator of the Tarzan series, which is simply a Daiquiri with Cointreau as the sweetener. Also, check out the Siesta, invented by Katie Stipe in 2006 at the Flatiron Lounge in Manhattan—it contains tequila, lime and grapefruit juices, simple syrup, and Campari. And while we're in New York City, bartender Amanda Bender invented yet another superb take on the Hemingway at a spot in Brooklyn called Names. It's the Six-Toed Cat, named for the polydactyl cats that now live at the Hemingway House in Key West. It pairs yuzu juice with white rum, and uses fresh lemon juice in place of lime juice.

For one last variation on the Daiquiri, I heartily recommend the Paddington, invented in the early 2000s by David Slape at the legendary East Village speakeasy PDT. It contains Banks 5 Island Rum, Lillet Blanc, grapefruit juice, lemon juice, orange juice, and absinthe.

DELICIOUS SOUR

New York City at the turn of the nineteenth century was a town full of what we today might call "rockstar bartenders." You'd see their names in the press all the time, for having invented this drink, serving that drink to that person, or creating something magical out of thin air. One such bartender was William "the Only William" Schmidt. I mean, having a nickname like "the Only William" just reeks of him being a diva, right? But the press loved him. An 1893 story in the *Philadelphia Inquirer* noted that Schmidt's new book, *The Flowing Bowl*, "has made him famous," and describes him as "several years in advance of the times. William invents a new drink every day." A 1904 piece in the *New York Times* gushed that Schmidt had created "a Mixture with Astonishing Qualities," which was "his masterpiece—the grand cocktail!" Newspapers spilled gallons and gallons of purple ink on his exploits.

Especially in his obituary, the love affair with the press continued. The *Greenville News* of January 12, 1905, stated that "he was the king of all bartenders, peerless and beyond compare in his profession. He made of bartending a fine art. Clad in his spotless white jacket and apron he was a monarch holding court . . . a smiling, kindly, gracious sovereign showering a sunshine of cordial courtesy and good will on all who came for his ministrations. Perhaps some part of this sunshine got into the divine concoctions he mixed." And so it went.

Which is not to say that he wasn't a great bartender, or that he didn't make some fine drinks. The Delicious Sour is just that, a delicious Sour. And it allows the reader to alter the ratios to perhaps dial it back a wee bit on the peach brandy or liqueur (as it can overpower). The recipe below is adapted from the 1896 edition of *Schmidt's Fancy Drinks and Popular Beverages: How to Prepare and Serve Them*. The original formulation calls for equal parts applejack and peach brandy, a "split-base" of spirits. But don't go running off to the store to purchase today's peach brandy since most available brandies are way too sweet (they're more like peach liqueurs, with sweetness added). But if you *can* get a true peach eau-de-vie, with no added sweetening, go with that.

recipe continues →

IF YOU'RE USING A (SWEET-ISH) PEACH LIQUEUR OR A GOOD PEACH SCHNAPPS:

1½ ounces applejack, apple brandy, or Calvados

½ ounce peach liqueur (such as Massenez crème de peche)

1 ounce fresh lime juice

1 medium egg white

¾ ounce soda water

IF YOU'RE USING A TRUE (UNSWEETENED) PEACH BRANDY OR EAU-DE-VIE:

1½ ounces applejack, apple brandy, or Calvados

1½ ounces peach brandy (such as Catoctin Creek or High Wire)

1 ounce fresh lime juice

1 medium egg white

⅓ ounce simple syrup (see page 6)

¾ ounce soda water

Combine the applejack, peach liqueur or brandy, lime juice, egg white, and simple syrup (if using) in a shaker without ice and dry shake (see page 4), then add ice and shake well for 15 seconds. Strain into a chilled cocktail glass. Rinse the shaker (see page 5) with the soda water, then strain the soda water into the glass.

DOUGLAS FAIRBANKS

Hollywood has always had a fascination with power couples, from Bogie and Bacall to Frank and Ava to Brad and Angelina . . . the list goes on. But perhaps the original power couple in Tinseltown was Douglas Fairbanks and Mary Pickford (see page 142). As silent films transitioned to talkies in the 1920s, Fairbanks and Pickford were arguably the king and queen of Hollywood. In 1919, they cofounded United Artists (with D. W. Griffith and Charlie Chaplin; see page 142), which for years was one of the largest and most successful entertainment companies in the world. Fairbanks starred in some of the earliest screen classics, notably *The Mark of Zorro, Robin Hood,* and *The Three Musketeers,* playing the quintessential swashbuckling hero in each. According to François Monti's excellent book *101 Cocktails to Try Before You Die,* both the Douglas Fairbanks and Mary Pickford cocktails were created by bartender Fred Kaufman, "a Brit who spoke English with a Spanish accent," at the Sevilla Biltmore Hotel in Havana during the 1920s. Curiously, you'll find two different versions of the Douglas Fairbanks being made at the same Havana bar! In the *Sloppy Joe's* cocktail book from 1931–32, it's made with equal parts rye and apricot liqueur, lime juice, and egg white; in the 1932–33 edition, it's a 2:1 mix of gin and apricot, along with the lime juice and egg white. We'll go with the latter recipe. Cheers to the Golden Era of Hollywood!

makes 1 cocktail

2 ounces gin

1 ounce apricot brandy

1 ounce fresh lime juice

1 medium egg white

Combine all the ingredients in a cocktail shaker without ice and dry shake (see page 4) to emulsify the egg white, then add ice and shake well again. Strain into a chilled cocktail glass.

ELIXIR OF COGNAC

This cocktail was invented in 2010 by H. Joseph Ehrmann, owner of the world-famous Elixir Saloon in San Francisco and one of the leaders of the Bay Area's craft cocktail scene. He invented it on the fly one day when "Pierre Ferrand, owner/distiller/blender, Alexandre Gabriel and national sales director Guillaume Lamy were visiting and sitting at the bar at Elixir." It's a classic Sour cocktail, with the egg white adding a creamy texture and the crème de cassis and pineapple syrup offering additional flavors and nuance.

makes 1 cocktail

1½ ounces Pierre Ferrand Ambre Cognac

½ ounce crème de cassis

½ ounce Small Hand Foods Pineapple Gum Syrup

1 ounce fresh lemon juice

1 ounce egg white

1 orange twist, for garnish

Combine the Cognac, crème de cassis, pineapple gum syrup, lemon juice, and egg white in a cocktail shaker without ice and dry shake (see page 4), then add ice and shake well again. Strain into an Old-Fashioned glass filled with ice and garnish with the orange twist.

variation: H. Joseph Ehrmann invented a companion to this drink: By substituting Irish whiskey for the Cognac, you've got a Kilkenny Sour.

FAR EAST GIMLET

My good friend Naren Young created this drink while he was creative director of Dante in New York City's East Village (he's now down in Miami, somehow managing both Sweet Liberty and Medium Cool). He wanted to create a Japanese riff on the classic Gimlet (page 99), using shōchū, a clear Japanese spirit distilled from sweet potatoes, barley, or rice. He split the original Gimlet's gin base with the shōchū and created his own lime cordial using only the zest and a little salt, and replaced the lime juice component with yuzu juice. He added a little spice with a bit of wasabi. The result is sublime.

makes 1 cocktail

1 ounce London dry gin

1 ounce shōchū

¾ ounce Salted Lime Syrup (recipe follows)

½ ounce yuzu juice (see page 13)

Pinch of wasabi powder or paste

½ teaspoon rice vinegar

1 fresh shiso leaf or mint leaf, for garnish

Combine the gin, shōchū, salted lime syrup, yuzu juice, wasabi, and vinegar in a cocktail shaker filled with ice and shake well. Strain into a chilled cocktail glass and garnish with the shiso leaf.

recipe continues →

SALTED LIME SYRUP

3 limes

½ cup sugar

1½ teaspoons Maldon sea salt

Using a Y-peeler, peel the limes, being careful to take only the green portion of the peel and not the bitter white albedo (pith). In a small saucepan, combine ½ cup water and the sugar and bring to a simmer over medium-high heat. Add the peels and the salt, remove from the heat, and let stand until the mixture is cool. Strain into an airtight container, then cover and refrigerate. It will keep for up to 1 month.

FAVOURITE SOUR

I was lucky enough to live and work in Wellington, New Zealand, a few years back, and during my time there I got to know a bunch of great folks in the cocktail world down under. Sebastian Reaburn is among them, and we've managed to keep in touch over the years. Based in Melbourne, Australia, he's now the master distiller at Top Shelf International and one of Australia's leading lights in the drinks industry. I asked him for one of his favorite Sours, and here's his entry. Sebastian loves gin sours and wanted to use apricot liqueur as an homage to a mentor he worked with in London in 2000, Mike Porter, who trained with the legendary Peter Dorelli at the Savoy back in the 1980s. Peter loved the Apricot Sour; it was his go-to cocktail. In the summer he shakes these without the aquafaba or egg white, because when the cocktail is light and foamy, it doesn't hit the palate with that sharp icy-cold zing. But in the winter, with plenty of foam, "this drinks like a liquid lemon meringue," he tells me. "The 'Favourite' in the name refers to whichever liqueur or fruit syrup you add—pick your favorite fruit to bring this cocktail to life! Cheers, mate!"

makes 1 cocktail

1¼ ounces Anther Gin (or any good London dry gin)

½ ounce bianco vermouth

1 ounce fresh lemon juice

½ ounce apricot liqueur (see Note)

¼ ounce aquafaba (see page 10) or egg white

1 lemon peel, for garnish

Combine the gin, vermouth, lemon juice, apricot liqueur, and aquafaba in a cocktail shaker without ice and dry shake (see page 4), then add ice and shake again. Strain into a chilled cocktail glass. As Sebastian says, "You can strain off the ice and 'dry shake' again if you are keen for it to be extra fluffy." Garnish with the lemon peel.

recipe continues →

note: Sebastian notes, "You can swap in your favourite fruit liqueur, or what you have on the shelf. Anything rich with plenty of sweetness will balance well. If you go for something a little lighter or drier, then add a splash of simple syrup to balance. You can even swap out the liqueur entirely for a fruit syrup."

FLORODORA

I learned about this delightful drink while reading the 2015 edition of my friend David Wondrich's essential book *Imbibe!*, in which he referenced a hit musical comedy on Broadway in 1900 that portrayed the misadventures of six lovely ladies on the fictitious island of Florodora in the Philippines. To say that the show was racy for its time might be an understatement. As Wondrich noted, "The 'Florodora Sextette' was hot, hot stuff."

But what about the drink? Newspaper accounts from July 1901 tell us that it was "the latest summer drink," and that "there is somewhat of romance in the tale of the way it was invented." Indeed, the *New York Evening World* describes an evening after a performance when "a party of professional people," including one of the chorus girls from the show, were at a Columbus Avenue restaurant in New York City. While everyone else in the group was tippin' 'em back, the chorus girl would drink only lemonade, which "irked the rest" of the party. Well, *yeah*.

Her friends twisted and twisted and twisted her arm, and she finally relented, saying to the bartender, Jimmy O'Brien, "If you'll get me something brand-new, I'll drink it." Ol' Jimmy "thought until the noise of his thinking drowned the whir of the electric fans." He then "turned out" the drink recipe shown below. And there was much rejoicing.

makes 1 cocktail

1½ ounces Plymouth gin (or London dry gin)

3 or 4 dashes raspberry syrup

1 ounce fresh lime juice

3 to 4 ounces ginger ale

1 orange wheel, for garnish

1 cocktail cherry, for garnish

recipe continues →

Combine the gin, raspberry syrup, and lime juice in a tall glass filled with ice. Add the ginger ale and stir. Garnish with the orange wheel and cherry.

variations: Use Cognac instead of gin and now you've got a Florodora Imperial Style (Wondrich, however, believes that calling it "Imperial Style" means you're also supposed to replace the ginger ale with Champagne). Or try rum as your base, use lemon juice instead of lime juice, add 1 teaspoon simple syrup, and use either soda water or ginger ale, and now it's a Boston Cooler. Or try applejack as your base and hard cider as your fizzy component, which results in a Stone Fence or Stonewall Jackson.

FOLK ART

This drink was created by DC bartender Sarah Rosner, who runs her own consultancy called Swill Merchants Co. She was inspired by another cocktail called the Art of Choke, created circa 2008 by Kyle Davidson for that great Chicago bar, the Violet Hour. That drink's name refers to the fact that it contains the artichoke-flavored aperitivo Cynar. Sarah created the Folk Art in 2014 while working at Eat the Rich in Washington, DC, and told me, "It was the first cocktail I was really stoked to call my own. In 2016, I included it in the interview for my first lead bar job, completely unaware that the man interviewing me was from Chicago *and* had worked at the Violet Hour."

makes 1 cocktail

4 or 5 mint leaves, plus 1 mint sprig for garnish

1 ounce Rhum Barbancourt 5 Star 8 year

1 ounce Cynar

½ ounce green Chartreuse (see Note, page 125)

½ ounce fresh lime juice

1 ounce pineapple juice

¼ ounce simple syrup (see page 6)

Slap the mint leaves against your palm to release some of their oils. Combine the mint leaves, rhum, Cynar, Chartreuse, lime juice, pineapple juice, and simple syrup in a cocktail shaker filled with ice and shake well. Strain into an Old-Fashioned glass filled with ice and garnish with "an artfully positioned mint sprig."

FOG CUTTER

I could certainly fill this book with tiki classics (since just about all of them are based on the Sour), but I had to include this one as it's one of my favorites. It might be one of the first split-base tiki drinks out there, meaning it has gin and brandy in addition to the rum. The name comes from a special knife used by scuba divers. The recipe is found in Victor "Trader Vic" Bergeron's entertaining 1947 *Bartender's Guide by Trader Vic*. In the 1972 edition of the book, Vic is quoted as saying, "Fog Cutter, hell. After two of these, you won't even see the stuff." But did Vic invent the drink? That's another matter.

In the deluxe edition of the 2009 book *Vintage Spirits and Forgotten Cocktails*, Ted "Dr. Cocktail" Haigh attempted to clear the fog away from this drink. It seems that bartender Tony Ramos invented an early Fogcutter (as Dr. Cocktail spells it) at Madame Wu's Chinese restaurant in Santa Monica, but Ramos also remembered another version of the drink being made at a joint called "Edna Fogcutter's" in Hollywood, at La Brea and Hollywood Boulevard. During his tenure at Madame Wu's, it appears that Ramos kept his Fogcutter recipe a strict secret. That said, Haigh visited Ramos during the 2000s when Ramos was working at Ciudad in downtown Los Angeles and got him to spill the beans: "I, Dr. Cocktail, brought my resources to bear and was able to extract the special recipe from the inimitable Ramos, published for the first time here." Since Ramos used commercial sweet-and-sour mix, I'm offering a modified version of the recipe herein.

1 ounce white rum

½ ounce London dry gin

½ ounce brandy

½ ounce fresh lemon juice

⅓ ounce simple syrup (see page 6)

1 teaspoon cherry brandy or kirsch, to float

Combine the rum, gin, brandy, lemon juice, and simple syrup in a blender with crushed ice and blend for 15 seconds. Pour into a goblet, then float (see page 5) the cherry brandy on top of the drink.

variation: Tiki authority Jeff "Beachbum" Berry notes that Don the Beachcomber served its own Fog Cutter: sweetened with orgeat, with pisco in place of the standard brandy, both lemon juice and orange juice, and topped with cream sherry, not cherry brandy.

FORTITUDE

I created this drink in honor of a seventy-ninth anniversary celebration of the 1944 D-Day invasion, held in the Cannon House Office Building on Capitol Hill, Washington, DC, on June 6, 2023. For the past ten years I've had the honor of serving as the bartender and toastmaster for the OSS Society, which celebrates the Office of Strategic Services (OSS), the US's intelligence and special operations agency during World War II, a predecessor to the Central Intelligence Agency. Over the years, I've created any number of military- and intelligence-themed drinks for their events—it's a cool gig. On this day, I wanted a drink to represent the contributions and sacrifices of the major play-ers on D-Day: the British (the gin), the Americans (the bourbon), the Canadians (the rye), and the French (the Calvados and Bénédictine). I also added lemon, to represent the bitter and sour fate of all of the brave souls who lost their lives that day. The name came from the tremendously successful deception campaign the Allies waged to keep the location and date of the invasion from the Nazis: Operation Fortitude.

Fortitude was a wide-ranging and fascinating operation. It featured fake (inflatable!) tanks and aircraft poised on the ground around Dover, England, so that German reconnaissance would believe the invasion would occur at Calais, France, directly across the English Channel. And the hiring of an actor who looked nearly identical to British Field Marshal Bernard Law Montgomery to parade around Northern Africa, to lead the Nazis into believing the invasion would be in the South of France! Cheers to Operation Fortitude!

1 ounce La Pommière Calvados

½ ounce Hayman's London dry gin

½ ounce Canadian rye whisky

½ ounce High Dive bourbon whiskey (or any quality bourbon)

½ ounce Bénédictine

½ ounce fresh lemon juice

Combine all the ingredients in a cocktail shaker filled with ice. Shake well and strain into a chilled cocktail glass.

FRENCH 75

This drink gets its name from a 75mm French-made artillery piece that was used extensively by the French and American armies during World War I (1914–1918) against the Germans. Ironically, what did the German officer order at Rick's Café Américain in the 1943 film *Casablanca*? A French 75, of course. His date, Yvonne, who'd been jilted by Rick (Humphrey Bogart) in an earlier scene, asks the bartender to "put up a whole row of those, Sascha, starting here and ending here." Perhaps in order for a French girl to get through a date with a Nazi, she needed a few strong drinks.

Indeed, the French 75 has long been known as a powerful drink. In December 1937, gossip columnist Walter Winchell, in his "On Broadway" column, noted that "The 'French 75' is the most potent drink in town. It's made like a Tom Collins, except that you use champagne instead of soda. One drink and you start swinging at people twice your size." During World War I, humorist Irvin S. Cobb wrote, "I had my first of these in a dugout in the Argonne. I couldn't tell whether a shell or the drink hit me."

The drink was nominally first seen in newspapers in December 1915, but that was a very different drink. The *Portsmouth Daily Times* told of "the Soixante-Quinze cocktail—The French Seventy-Five. It is one-third gin, one-third grenadine, one-third applejack and a dash of lemon juice." Harry's New York Bar in Paris in the 1920s offered a similar recipe. Then, a 1927 cocktail book called *Here's How* was written under the nom de plume "Judge Jr." The author's real name was Norman Hume Anthony; he was a cartoonist and later became the editor of *Life* magazine. Perhaps because the book was published during Prohibition, he had to be dodgy about his identity. At any rate, his book offered the recipe we know today:

> This drink is really what won the War for the Allies:
> 2 jiggers Gordon water [*He means Gordon's London dry gin— again, that Prohibition-era dodginess!*]
> 1 part lemon juice
> 1 spoonful of powdered sugar; cracked ice.

Fill up the rest of a tall glass with champagne! (If you use club soda instead of champagne, you have a Tom Collins.)

Harry Craddock's *The Savoy Cocktail Book* (1930) essentially "codified" the *Here's How* recipe, and that's how the drink has been made ever since. Well, unless you're in New Orleans, that is. (How's that? See the sidebar on page 96 about how the drink is made in the City that Care Forgot.) As for the rest of the world, here's how to make a French 75.

makes 1 cocktail

2 ounces London dry gin

½ ounce fresh lemon juice

¾ ounce simple syrup (see page 6)

4 ounces chilled Champagne or sparkling wine

1 lemon peel, for garnish

Combine the gin, lemon juice, and simple syrup in a cocktail shaker filled with ice. Shake well and strain into a highball glass, wineglass, or flute filled with ice. Top the drink with the Champagne and garnish with the lemon peel.

variations: If you use Cointreau in place of the simple syrup, you've made a Flying cocktail, a favorite of Ian Fleming in his twenties. He likely encountered the drink while at university in Munich, where it was invented by bartender Conrad Rosenow. Or use light rum in place of the gin and honey syrup as the sweetener and you've made an Air Mail, a Cuban classic that Bacardí promoted vigorously in the 1930s. There's also the Calvados 75—basically a French 75 with Calvados or applejack as the spirit—created by Sasha Petraske of Milk & Honey in the 2000s. Or try the Seaplane, a French 75 with an absinthe-rinsed glass and some orange bitters, invented by Joseph Schwartz, also at Milk & Honey.

THE FRENCH 75, N'AWLINS (AND MID-CENTURY) STYLE

When it comes to the French 75, there's the gin version—how it's made in most parts of the globe—and then there's the way it's made in New Orleans, where they don't see the sense in making a French drink with an English spirit (hard to argue with that, *mon Dieu!*). At the French 75 Bar at world-famous Arnaud's restaurant (and elsewhere), it's made with Cognac, not gin.

Chris Hannah, former head bartender at Arnaud's (who now has his own place in the Quarter, Jewel of the South), was the one responsible for the Cognac version at the French 75 Bar (circa 2004) and the creation and promotion of the narrative that the drink was always made that way down in the French Quarter.

It appears that Chris heard about the Cognac version on Dick Shepard's syndicated radio show, and he also knew that Arnaud's then-owner, Archie Casbarian Sr., made his French 75 that way. Chris also believes that Arnaud's founder, "Count" Arnaud Cazenave, was a Cognac guy (of course he was, he was originally a French wine salesman!). All of this planted a seed in Chris to create the narrative that the French 75 was *always* made with Cognac in New Orleans. Now, twenty years later, the "myth" has elevated to "fact." It *is* how the drink is made in New Orleans. Bravo, Mr. Hannah!

But is this method of making the French 75 with Cognac exclusive to New Orleans? Perhaps not. If you go back to the middle of the last century, you'll find plenty of examples when it's squarely a Cognac (or brandy) drink. For example, American actress Tallulah Bankhead was an aficionado of the Cognac/brandy version.

It's also worth noting that David Embury offered but one way to make a French 75: with Cognac. (That said, he noted that "gin is sometimes used in place of Cognac in this drink, but then it should no longer be called French.")

There are other instances of the French 75 being made with Cognac in that era. The *San Francisco Examiner* of February 6, 1952, cheekily advised readers, "Speaking of the high cost of hangovers, the Mark [now the Intercontinental Mark Hopkins Hotel] has just ooped [*sic*] the tariff on its French 75s [champagne and cognac] to $1.60, and proudly announced that it's 'our most expensive drink,' swellll. . . ." And on December 23, 1952, the *Baltimore Sun* succinctly noted, "A 'World War II French '75' calls for 1 jigger of cognac to a glass of champagne." And lastly, when Charles de Gaulle made a visit to San Francisco in late April 1960, the *San Francisco Examiner* suggested that the locals enjoy a French 75 to "honor President de Gaulle . . . by drinking a French 75. Three oz. French Champagne, three-fourths oz French Cognac, and after such oz. you are guaranteed to feel like Dorothy in a windstorm."

One final note: Some folks have opted to avoid the whole "gin or Cognac" tempest in a flute glass by calling the Cognac/brandy version the "French 125." According to Simon Difford, the drink is named for another artillery piece, the 2A46, a 125mm howitzer developed in the 1960s for the Soviet Union's Red Army. The earliest-known instances where the Cognac version was listed as the French 125 was in *Jones' Complete Barguide* in 1977, by Stanley M. Jones. And for what it's worth, that same book has the bourbon version of the drink going by the name French 95.

FRENCH SQUIRREL

In the first edition of *The Joy of Mixology*, Gary Regan had a comprehensive system of drink categories (see page 28). Among them were "Squirrel Sours," a name apparently of his own making. He considered them to be "a whole new genre of cocktails, and it's a result of [his then-wife] Mardee insisting that we buy some crème de noyau, a pink, almond-flavored liqueur." Regan made Mardee a drink he called the Pretty in Pink, and it sparked an idea: "Suppose I substitute crème de noyau for the triple sec in some of the New Orleans sours?" He began playing around with other nut-based liqueurs (Get it? Squirrels eat nuts!), such as Frangelico, Nocello, and amaretto, and "a new category was born."

The French Squirrel was the favorite in the category, said Regan, and "truly lends itself to experimentation with other nut-flavored liqueurs." Regan omitted the discussion of Squirrel Sours, and this drink, from the revised edition of *The Joy of Mixology*. I recently asked his dear friend David Wondrich if he had any idea why Regan did this, and Wondrich responded, "I sure wish he was around so we could ask him." Truer words were never spoken.

makes 1 cocktail

2 ounces Cognac

½ ounce crème de noyaux

½ ounce fresh lemon juice

1 lemon twist, for garnish

Combine the Cognac, crème de noyaux, and lemon juice in a cocktail shaker filled with ice and shake well. Strain into a chilled cocktail glass and garnish with the lemon twist.

variation: To make a Pretty in Pink, use Van Gogh Wild Appel vodka in place of the Cognac, shake, and strain into an ice-filled Collins glass, then top with a little soda water and garnish with a lemon twist.

GIMLET

After the Bay of Pigs fiasco, president John F. Kennedy somberly noted, "Success has many fathers, but failure is an orphan." The same is true with classic cocktails, it seems. Name me a drink where we can agree who invented it (such as the Vieux Carré, invented by Walter Bergeron at the Hotel Monteleone in New Orleans, circa 1934), and I'll give you many others where we may have no clear idea, but there's a list of people getting the credit (see the Cosmopolitan, Martini, Manhattan, Sidecar, Bloody Mary, et al.). The Gimlet is another one.

One popular story concerns a Royal Navy surgeon, Sir Thomas D. Gimlette, who encouraged men at sea to mix lime juice with gin, around 1880. It's certainly plausible, given the British Navy's penchant for mixing citrus with their daily ration of gin or rum (see the Navy Grog, page 162). Then again, there's no reference to this accomplishment in his obituary. But in a somewhat related vein, in his excellent contribution to *The Oxford Companion to Spirits and Cocktails*, my friend Paul Clarke tells us that "the Gimlet's genesis began with the passage of the Merchant Shipping Act of 1867, which mandated that British merchant ships stock rations of lime juice to prevent scurvy; the same year, Lauchlan Rose (1829–1855) patented an alcohol-free process of preserving lime juice, and Rose's Lime Juice Cordial was soon widely distributed."

But there's also the fact that a small handheld drilling or boring tool called a "gimlet" is what a Royal Navy sailor would use to make an opening in a cask or barrel containing spirits. Could this be the drink name's origin? It's anyone's guess.

Further, this is one of those cocktails that have both an "authentic" way to make it, and a "better" way to make it, which sounds odd but here goes: To make an authentic Gimlet, you need to use Rose's Lime Juice Cordial (now called Rose's Sweetened Lime Juice). But let's face it—today's Rose's, while "authentic" to the recipe, contains high-fructose corn syrup, lime juice concentrate, and artificial coloring. Folks, we can do better. It's called squeezing

recipe continues →

the juice of half a lime (or so) and mixing some sugar and water to make simple syrup (page 6); or purchasing or making a good lime cordial (see page 9).

The Gimlet has played a role in the pages of literature as well as the small screen. Hemingway featured Gimlets in *Green Hills of Africa*, as well as in "The Short Happy Life of Francis Macomber." David Mamet's Pulitzer Prize–winning play *Glengarry Glen Ross* has multiple scenes wherein desperate, down-on-their-luck Chicago real estate agents are tossin' back Gimlets while trying to make a sale or bemoaning their lack of good leads ("Gimlets are for closers"?). You'll also find Gregory Peck and Ava Gardner drinking them in the 1952 film *The Snows of Kilimanjaro*, which is based on the Hemingway short story (where, oddly enough, it does *not* appear). And the drink nearly has a starring role in Raymond Chandler's classic noir thriller *The Long Goodbye* (1953):

> We sat in a corner of the bar at Victor's and drank gimlets. "They don't know how to make them here," he said. "What they call a gimlet is just some lime or lemon juice with a dash of sugar and bitters. A real gimlet is half gin and half Rose's Lime Juice and nothing else. It beats martinis hollow.

And in season 1, episode 2 of *Mad Men*, a tipsy and soon-to-be-ill Betty Draper sardonically observes that "Lobster Newburg and Gimlets should get a divorce. They're not getting along very well." Yet the drink remained her favorite through the whole series. Whichever way you make it, with fresh juice and simple syrup, with Rose's in the 1:1 Chandler manner, or the recipe shown here, it's a classic. Here's how.

2 ounces London dry gin

¾ ounce fresh lime juice mixed with ½ ounce simple syrup (see page 6),
   or 1 ounce Rose's Sweetened Lime Juice

Combine all the ingredients in a cocktail shaker filled with ice. Shake well and strain into a chilled cocktail glass.

variations: Use vodka to make a Vodka Gimlet. Or add 2 dashes of Angostura bitters to the classic gin-based Gimlet and blend it all with crushed ice, and you've got a Rangoon Gimlet, created in 1963 by legendary tiki bartender Tony Ramos at the China Trader, in what television announcer Gary Owens (*Rowan & Martin's Laugh-In*) used to call "beautiful downtown Burbank," California. For a Japanese twist, try the Far East Gimlet (page 83), or the Jackson Pollock (page 116) for a lime-and-grapefruit Gimlet with an amazing garnish.

GIN FIZZ

This classic dates to the nineteenth century and has been a favorite of so many notable figures. F. Scott and Zelda Fitzgerald loved the drink but were characteristically careless when they allowed their little daughter to enjoy one, too. He later wrote, "We bathed the daughter in the bidet by mistake and she drank the gin fizz thinking it was lemonade and ruined the luncheon table next day." Hmm, to have been a fly on the wall at that luncheon . . . Also, in a 1929 Dorothy Parker short story in *The New Yorker* we find the Fizz down on the Côte d'Azur: "The two young New Yorkers sat on the cool terrace that rose sharp from the Mediterranean, and looked into deep gin fizzes, embellished, in the Riviera manner, with mint."

Dr. Thomas More, the protagonist of Walker Percy's 1971 novel *Love in the Ruins*, enjoys more Ramos Gin Fizzes than one can count during a country club Christmas party, dangerously tempting fate (ahem, *he just might be allergic to egg whites!*). But who cares? He's in love with the fabulously tall and gorgeous Lola: "I see her clearly, gin fizz in one hand, the other held against her sacrum, palm out, pushing herself rhythmically off the wall. Women! Music! Love! Life! Joy! Gin fizzes!" He loses control: "Trays pass. I begin to drink Ramos gin fizzes with one swallow. At one time I was allergic to egg white but that was long ago. These drinks feel silky and benign." Well, benign they weren't; he ends up passing out in a greenside bunker, probably in anaphylactic shock, and it takes a shot of epinephrine to save his life!

But it's probably Senator Huey Long, the Louisiana Kingfish, who offers the most entertaining Gin Fizz story. In July 1935, Huey went up to New York City to meet with some Wall Street types. He sampled a Ramos at the bar of the New Yorker Hotel and found it lacking. So, he arranged to have Sam Guarino, the head bartender at Huey's beloved Roosevelt Hotel in New Orleans, fly up to Manhattan to teach the locals how to properly make a Ramos Gin Fizz. It became a publicity stunt; with newsreel cameras rolling, Huey and Sam made one Ramos after another until the bar staff at the New Yorker "mastered the proposition." Huey insisted on "sampling" the finished product. He told the hotel's manager, "As you know I haven't had a drink in eighteen months but I'll sample this, Ralph, in order to be able to assure you that it's genuine." (He takes a long pull.) "I think that's all right. I *think* that's all right. Better be sure about it." He ended up drinking six of them! You know, to be absolutely sure they were *gen-u-wine*.

Let's start out with the classic Gin Fizz recipe, then I'll tell you about some of the amazing variations on this great little drink. (The basic Gin Fizz is essentially the same drink as the Tom Collins, but served up and not on the rocks.)

makes 1 cocktail

2 ounces London dry gin

½ ounce fresh lemon juice

½ ounce simple syrup (see page 6)

2 to 3 ounces chilled soda water

1 lime wheel, for garnish (optional)

Combine the gin, lemon juice, and simple syrup in a cocktail shaker filled with ice. Shake well and strain into a chilled cocktail glass. Add the soda water, stir, and garnish with the lime wheel, if desired.

variation: The Ramos Gin Fizz is perhaps the best-known Gin Fizz. It was invented circa 1888 by Henry Charles Ramos at his bar, the Imperial Cabinet. He later moved to the Stag Saloon just down the street. Here, the Ramos Gin Fizz became legendary. In his colorful 1937 book *Famous New Orleans Drinks and How to Mix 'Em*, Stanley Clisby Arthur noted that during the 1917 Mardi Gras season, Ramos had to hire thirty-five "shaker boys" who "nearly shook their arms off, but were still unable to keep up with the demand."

Ramos himself was quoted in a 1928 issue of the *New Orleans Item-Tribune* as saying that you need to "shake and shake and shake until there is not a bubble left but the drink is smooth and snowy white and of the consistency of good rich milk." Indeed, he shook the drink with the soda water in it! Me, I shake the Ramos for about three minutes, but some bartenders go six, and some wise ones use a blender!

RAMOS GIN FIZZ

makes 1 cocktail

1½ ounces London dry gin (however, you could use
   Old Tom gin since that's likely what Ramos used)

½ ounce fresh lemon juice

½ ounce fresh lime juice

1 ounce heavy cream

½ ounce simple syrup (see page 6)

3 or 4 drops orange flower water

1 medium egg white

2 to 3 ounces soda water

Combine all the ingredients in a cocktail shaker with 1 large ice cube. Shake well, then strain into a short highball glass. Savor it. As Stanley Clisby Arthur wrote, "It's like drinking a flower."

HOTEL NACIONAL SPECIAL

The enactment of the Volstead Act, which brought about Prohibition in 1920, caused a great "brain drain" of talented bartenders who, in an instant, found that pursuing their career in their own country had become illegal. One of those bartenders was Eddie Woelke (see the Madison Avenue, page 134), who had previously tended bar at the Knickerbocker Hotel, the Biltmore, and Delmonico's in New York, as well as the Plaza Athénée in Paris. As was noted in the *Brooklyn Daily Eagle* on October 2, 1936, "When prohibition put its blight on legal conviviality here, Eddie went to Havana's Seville Biltmore, became known as the only bartender to serve more than one million cocktails made of Bacardí." One of them was the Hotel Nacional Special.

Woelke would later move to Havana's Hotel Nacional, and his connection to Bacardí continued. The Nacional was, along with the Hotel Ambos Mundos, among the premier hotels in Cuba's capital. Ernest Hemingway was an occasional guest at the hotel but, curiously, he did his drinking elsewhere. In fact, he wrote to his then wife, Martha Gellhorn, in 1943, "Everything is lovely here at the Nacional and the only thing lacking is you dear if you could only see the view from my room looking out over the beautiful Gulf Stream and oh those daiquiris that nobody makes like old Constantino"—referring to Constante Ribalaigua at the nearby El Floridita (see the Daiquiri, page 75).

Curiously, in his 1939 book *The Gentleman's Companion: Vol. II, Being an Exotic Drinking Book; Or, Around the World with Jigger, Beaker, and Flask*, Charles H. Baker Jr. stated rather emphatically that the Hotel Nacional was invented by Wil P. Taylor, the manager of the Nacional. The recipe is essentially the same, but as Jeff "Beachbum" Berry noted in *The Oxford Companion to Spirits and Cocktails*, Taylor's recipe "lacks the balance of Woelke's." As I've said before, success has many fathers.

recipe continues →

1½ ounces white rum

1½ ounces pineapple juice

¼ ounce fresh lime juice

¼ ounce apricot brandy

1 cocktail cherry, for garnish

Combine the rum, pineapple juice, lime juice, and brandy in a cocktail shaker filled with ice and shake well. Strain into a chilled cocktail glass. Garnish with the cherry.

HURRICANE

Ah, there's nothing quite like the experience of sitting in the courtyard at Pat O'Brien's in the French Quarter of New Orleans, sitting by the flaming fountain and sipping on a Hurricane. If only the drink was as good as it *could* be. Sadly, Pat O's is stuck in the 1980s with their artificially flavored, artificially colored ingredients. They'll even sell you their powdered or bottled Hurricane Mix. Powdered mixes that are truly abominable! I mean, Tang powdered orange drink is great if you're, you know, an Apollo astronaut heading to the Moon, or a backpacker who can't handle the extra weight. But would you make a mimosa with Tang? No. We can do better

Pat O's claims that the Hurricane was invented out of necessity, that during World War II there were shortages of things like whiskey (because US distillers were producing more alcohol for the war effort and didn't have the capacity to meet demand for beverage spirits). But there was plenty of rum coming into New Orleans from our Latin American trading partners. Distributors would insist that if a bar wanted to buy whiskey, they'd have to also buy X number of bottles of rum for every bottle of whiskey. So, O'Brien decided to make a rum drink that could burn up all that rum he had on hand. The drink was introduced in 1942 and was "expensive" for its day: sixty cents. O'Brien explained that it was expensive because it had 4 ounces of rum in it! According to my friend (and fellow cocktail historian) Cheryl Charming, the original 1942 recipe was 4 ounces of rum, with lime juice, orange juice, and passionfruit syrup served in a 22-ounce "hurricane" glass (so called because it resembled the chimney on a lantern that kept a candle lit even on a windy day). If only they still made them that way!

The only problem with that story is that I have in my collection a little cock-tail recipe book printed by the Ronrico Rum Co. called *The Rum Connoisseur*. Within the pages of this tiny gem is the recipe shown below. So what's so important about this discovery? It has a copyright date of 1941, and the United States only entered World War II in December of that year! As such, it seems the Ronrico recipe predates Pat O'Brien's purported invention of the drink. There's one other claim out there, that the Hurricane was invented at Webb

Lake Motel up in Wisconsin in the 1930s, which was operated by one Andrew Kucharski. As that story goes, the owners of Pat O's "discovered" the drink at the motel's bar and brought it back to New Orleans with them, declaring it to be their own invention.

makes 1 cocktail

RONRICO'S HURRICANE PUNCH

1 ounce fresh lime juice

1 ounce fresh lemon juice

2 ounces passion fruit syrup (Monin makes a nice one, but you might want to start with just 1 ounce so as not to make it too sweet)

4 ounces dark rum (for authenticity's sake, use Ronrico Gold Label, but any good dark rum, especially a Jamaican rum, is fine)

1 orange slice, for garnish

2 cherries, for garnish

Combine the lime juice, lemon juice, passion fruit syrup, and rum in a blender filled with crushed ice. Blend for 15 seconds, then pour the drink into a Hurricane glass. (Alternatively, simply combine the ingredients in a cocktail shaker filled with ice, shake well, and strain into the glass.) Garnish with the orange slice and cherries and serve with a straw.

IDEAL

This classic can be found in cocktail books going back to World War I, with its earliest-known mention in the pages of Hugo Ensslin's 1917 *Recipes for Mixed Drinks*. And, although better known for his suite of Daiquiris (page 75), Constante Ribalaigua also made the Ideal (it's pronounced *iddy-al*, by the way) one of the house specialties at El Floridita in Havana. The recipe shown below is found in El Floridita's cocktail recipe booklets in the late 1930s. It's a delicious drink that has aspects of the Martinez (which also features gin, maraschino liqueur, and vermouth) but with grapefruit to brighten it up and add some acidity. Or you might look at it as a riff on the Bronx or Queens cocktails, but with grapefruit in place of the orange (Bronx) or pineapple (Queens).

According to syndicated columnist Robert Ruark, it's the drink Ernest Hemingway would enjoy when he wasn't, you know, tossing back seventeen Papa Dobles in one sitting. Constante would serve a small bowl of almonds as an accompaniment to the drink, which I highly recommend.

makes 1 cocktail

1 ounce London dry gin

1 ounce dry vermouth

1 ounce sweet vermouth

¾ ounce grapefruit juice

1 teaspoon maraschino liqueur

Combine all the ingredients in a cocktail shaker filled with ice and shake well. Strain into a chilled cocktail glass.

ITALIAN FUSION FIZZ

This Collins-Fizz variation comes from my friend Mattia Pastori in Milan, Italy. Back in October 2016, two of our daughters happened to find themselves with an evening together in Milan, and asked their old man if he knew of any good places to eat and drink. I went to Facebook to ask my friends in the food and beverage world for advice, but for their privacy I was vague about whom the info was for. World-renowned spirits expert Giuseppe Gallo, at the time an award-winning brand ambassador for Martini & Rossi, tagged a couple of bartenders in Milan, and said, "Our dear friend Philip Greene is in town. Can you please look after him? Negroni time." Mattia then responded, "We're awaiting you at Damascegliere—shaker and glasses are really cold." Damascegliere, now closed, was at the time a great bar and restaurant, and it was literally in the same courtyard as my daughters' Airbnb (small world!). So they had a lovely dinner and drinks under Mattia's excellent hospitality (and it turned out he's also a fan of my Hemingway book—another small-world coincidence). As I often joke, my daughters and my books travel the world.

When I asked Mattia for a drink recipe, he offered a Fizz variation on a Negroni-style drink he'd invented recently, inspired by the Tokyo traditions of Sakura, the time of the cherry blossoms. He noted that the drink, "with the flavors of the almond and the hint of wild cherry in the bitters working really well together, and with the Italian tonic water, it gives extra bitterness to the drink."

Having left Damascegliere, Mattia is now the CEO and founder of Nonsolococktails, a consultancy, education, and events company in the hospitality sector, based in Milan. Coincidentally, the main component of the drink, Italicus Rosolio di Bergamotto, was created by Giuseppe Gallo, "to bring back the forgotten Rosolio category, once the main aperitivo drunk by the King of Savoia," according to the company website. So here you have Giuseppe introducing me to Mattia, who then uses Giuseppe's delightful product in his recipe. A small world sometimes just gets smaller, no? It's a great drink and I hope you enjoy!

1 ounce Italicus Rosolio di Bergamotto

⅔ ounce Marendry Amarena Fabbri

⅔ ounce sake

½ ounce yuzu juice (see page 13)

⅙ ounce almond milk

2 ounces Acqua Brillante Recoaro Tonica (or any good Italian tonic water)

1 grapefruit peel, for garnish

Combine the Italicus, Amarena Fabbri, sake, yuzu juice, and almond milk in a cocktail shaker filled with ice and shake well. Strain into a Collins glass filled with ice. Rinse the shaker (see page 5) with the tonic water, then strain the tonic into the glass. Garnish with the grapefruit peel.

THE FIZZ BIZ

Just as the Sour serves as an excellent platform for innovation, the Gin Fizz (page 102), also in that category, creates a similar phenomenon, and here are but a few:

- The Golden Fizz is a Gin Fizz, but with an egg yolk thrown into the mix.

- The Silver Fizz is a Gin Fizz, but with an egg white.

- The Royal Fizz, you guessed it, uses the entire egg.

- The Diamond Fizz? It has Champagne or sparkling wine in place of the soda water.

- The Hoffman House Fizz uses maraschino liqueur in place of the simple syrup, along with ½ ounce sweet cream and 1 teaspoon fresh orange juice.

- The Albemarle Fizz is a Gin Fizz but with ½ ounce raspberry syrup added after the drink is made.

- The Crimson Fizz is a Gin Fizz with a handful of crushed strawberries thrown into the shaker.

- The Alabama Fizz is a Gin Fizz garnished with several sprigs of mint.

- The Applejack Fizz is a Gin Fizz but with applejack or Calvados in place of the gin. Along these lines, you can make a Fizz with bourbon, brandy, rum, sloe gin, or whatever spirit you have on hand.

And now for something completely different (and low-alcohol), try the Angostura Fizz, aka the Trinidad Fizz: 1 ounce (!) Angostura bitters, ½ ounce of either fresh lemon juice or lime juice, 1 egg white, and ½ ounce heavy cream. Shake, then top with soda water.

Or try the Thai Canton Gin Fizz, which I invented circa 2008 when I was helping launch Domaine de Canton ginger liqueur: 2 ounces London dry gin, ½ ounce fresh lemon juice, ¾ ounce Domaine de Canton, and 3 basil leaves added to the shaker. Shake, then strain into a highball glass or flute and top with chilled soda water.

The Silver Fox is a Silver Fizz (see earlier in this list) with orgeat in place of the simple syrup, with the addition of a little amaretto. This modern classic was invented by Richard Boccato at Milk & Honey in the 2000s.

The New Orleans Gin Fizz is a Gin Fizz with the addition of ½ ounce fresh lime juice, 1 egg white, and ½ ounce heavy cream. Some versions of this drink contain Old Tom gin in place of the London dry.

JACK ROSE

For some years I believed (and even wrote) that the Jack Rose might have been named after New York City gangster Jacob Rosenzweig, who went by the nickname "Bald Jack" Rose. The poor guy had a bout with typhoid as a lad, which rendered him not only hairless but also the butt of schoolboy jokes and bullying. So he naturally channeled that rage into a life of crime. The American dream, right? Rose took part in a 1912 gangland assassination of mob boss Herman "Beansy" Rosenthal (gotta love those nicknames), and when Rose (perhaps falsely) testified that he was ordered to make the hit by a crooked cop, that cop went to the electric chair in 1915, while Rose walked. You can't make this stuff up!

Alas, that name origin story doesn't hold up to the facts. See, the drink appears in cocktail books that predate ol' Bald Jack's notoriety; it's first seen around the turn of the last century. Per David Wondrich's entry on the drink in *The Oxford Companion to Spirits and Cocktails*, it was likely invented by Frank Haas circa 1899 when he was working at Fred Eberlin's bar in New York City. There are other candidates, however. And as for the drink's name, it's likely either after the 'Général Jacqueminot' rose (which has lovely pink hue), or simply because it's made with applejack and is rose colored.

But it *is* truthful to say that the Jack Rose was *renamed* because of Bald Jack Rose. In the fallout of the assassination and ensuing trial, it was felt that the mobster's infamy had tarnished the drink's noble name. Thus the drink was (temporarily) renamed the Royal Smile. Thankfully, this only lasted a few years.

The recipe shown below is the "standard" recipe you'll find in most bars today. However, they did things a little (actually, a lot) differently in Paris back in the 1920s. At Harry's New York Bar, they started with the contemporary, three-part Jack Rose recipe shown below, then they added ¾ ounce each of orange juice and London dry gin, then ⅓ ounce each of sweet and dry vermouth. It's as if they took the Jack Rose and mashed it up with the Bronx Cocktail. And it's a pretty delicious drink (just a bear to make!). As such, I've made the argument that perhaps it was this more complicated

Jack Rose that Jake Barnes was drinking while waiting for Brett at the Hôtel Crillon, in Hemingway's 1926 novel *The Sun Also Rises*. Try them both and judge for yourself!

makes 1 cocktail

2 ounces applejack (Laird's Straight Apple Brandy is delightful) or Calvados

½ ounce fresh lemon or lime juice

¼ ounce grenadine

Combine all the ingredients in a cocktail shaker filled with ice. Shake well and strain into a chilled cocktail glass.

variations: Use Cointreau in place of the grenadine and add lemon juice, and you've made yourself an Apple Car. With lemon juice, simple syrup, and egg white (or aquafaba; see page 10), it's a Jersey Sour. Another delicious variation, invented by Sasha Petraske at Milk & Honey, is the Apple Jack, which contains applejack, apple cider, lemon juice, and simple syrup.

JACKSON POLLOCK
(AKA JACKSON SQUARE)

This drink was created by Nick Kosevich, an internationally renowned bar educator and consultant and cofounder of Bittercube, which specializes in handcrafted bitters. With a passion for creating unique and innovative drink experiences, he has gained recognition for his expertise in the world of craft cocktails. He also is co-owner and CEO of Earl Giles Distillery, and a partner at Mr. Paul's Supper Club in the Minneapolis suburb of Edina.

As for the drink's background, Nick tells me:

> The first time I made this drink was for Bombay Sapphire gin's "Most Imaginative Bartender" Competition in 2008, and it's stuck with me ever since. The drink's original name was the Jackson Pollock; it's sort of an homage to the great oil painter, and since the drink has two somewhat oily garnishes that move across the surface of the drink as you enjoy it, I thought it worked. It's since been featured on menus throughout the Twin Cities and currently resides on the menu at Mr. Paul's, under the name Jackson Square, in keeping with that restaurant's New Orleans–Louisiana theme. Colored oils as a garnish isn't a new idea now but it sure as hell felt that way back in 2008!

He goes on to say that while "the basil and paprika oils are a bit of a pain in the ass to make and the drink is as delicious without them, it's certainly not as pretty." It is a very tasty drink, absolutely, but the two-oil garnish takes it to another level. At its core, this is a simple but delicious variation on the classic Gimlet (page 99), with some grapefruit juice added to bring additional flavor and acidity.

2 ounces Earl Giles London Dry Gin (or any good London dry)

1½ ounces On the Fly Elixir (recipe follows)

2 dashes Bittercube Jamaican #2 bitters

1½ ounces Champagne or sparkling wine, to top

A few drops Basil Oil (recipe follows), for garnish

A few drops Paprika Oil (recipe follows), for garnish

Combine the gin, elixir, and bitters in a cocktail shaker filled with ice. Shake well and strain into a chilled cocktail glass. Top with the Champagne, then carefully add a few drops each of basil oil and paprika oil to the surface of the drink.

ON THE FLY ELIXIR

makes 2½ cups

7 ounces fresh grapefruit juice

3 ounces fresh lime juice

10 ounces simple syrup (see page 6)

Combine all the ingredients in an airtight container and stir. Cover and store in the refrigerator; it will keep for about a week.

recipe continues →

BASIL OIL

2 cups fresh basil leaves

1 cup extra-virgin olive oil

Bring 2 cups water to a boil in a small saucepan. Fill a bowl with ice and water and set it nearby. Add the basil leaves to the boiling water and blanch them for 10 seconds, then quickly transfer them to the ice water to stop the cooking process while maintaining their vibrant green color; let cool. Gently squeeze out any excess water from the basil leaves and transfer to a blender or food processor. Add the olive oil and blend until the mixture is smooth and well combined. If desired, strain the mixture through a fine-mesh sieve or cheesecloth (some people prefer a more rustic texture with bits of basil in the oil). Transfer the oil to a clean airtight container or bottle. Let cool, then store in the refrigerator to maintain its freshness and vibrant color. It will keep for at least a month.

PAPRIKA OIL

makes ½ cup

2 tablespoons sweet paprika

½ cup grapeseed oil

Combine the paprika and grapeseed oil in an airtight container or bottle and stir. Cover and store at room temperature. It will keep indefinitely.

JALISCIENCE

This delicious drink comes from my old pal Duane Sylvestre. Like me, Duane is a Washington, DC, native but also has deep roots in Trinidad. For the past twelve years or so, he's been working with brands like Rémy Cointreau and Campari, but before that he was one of DC's finest bartenders. Duane, Gina Chersevani (see page 225), and I have teamed up to present the annual (and super-popular) DC Holiday Craft Cocktail Seminar series, which features some of the best mixologists and storytellers from our nation's capital.

As for the drink, Duane explains that "it's still one of my favorites, and the name loosely translates to something from Jalisco," a state in western Mexico known for its tequila production. Duane further describes it as "a pleasant departure from the classic Sour or margarita, and it works great with a rhum agricole, too." He also noted that he invented it around 2009 while he was behind the stick at the acclaimed Bourbon Steak in the Four Seasons Hotel in Georgetown. He added:

> Jaliscience (pronounced *ha-lee-sea-ehn-say*) was one of the first cocktails added to the menu when we were given the independence to contribute toward the restaurant's beverage program. The grapefruit-ginger combination comes from two of my favorite beverages in Trinidad, namely, the ginger beer and the grapefruit juice drinks that are offered at many of the island's food parlors. I love how these flavors complement each other in this drink. Trust me when I say it hits different! Originally it was to be a rum-based cocktail, but I came to discover that it was better with agave. The name was coined by my good friend José-Luis O'Beristain. He is an old-school service professional who believes in simplicity with substance. Something from Jalisco was born.

recipe continues →

1½ ounces Cabo Wabo reposado tequila

½ ounce fresh lemon juice

½ ounce Ginger Syrup (recipe follows)

¾ ounce fresh grapefruit juice

1 grapefruit peel, for garnish

Combine the tequila, lemon juice, ginger syrup, and grapefruit juice in a cocktail shaker filled with ice. Shake well and strain into a chilled cocktail glass (or, as an alternative, an Old-Fashioned glass filled with ice). Garnish with the grapefruit peel.

GINGER SYRUP   *makes 2 cups*

⅔ cup ginger juice (use bottled ginger juice or a food processor to puree the ginger root)

1 cup granulated sugar

¼ cup Demerara sugar or brown sugar

In a small saucepan, combine ⅓ cup water, the ginger juice, granulated sugar, and Demerara sugar. Heat over medium heat, stirring, until the sugars have dissolved. Let cool, then strain into an airtight container. Cover and store in the refrigerator. It will keep for several weeks.

JUNGLE BIRD

I love the backstory of this drink almost as much as I love the drink. And I *adore* the drink. While the Jungle Bird has become a fixture in the craft and tiki cocktail scenes over the past fifteen or so years, it was for several decades unknown outside of its birthplace in Malaysia. One of the house drinks at the Aviary Bar at the Kuala Lumpur Hilton in the late 1970s, the Jungle Bird had been created by bartender Jeffrey Ong to give as a greeting to guests arriving at the hotel. But, like so many such "house drinks," it was known only to a few.

The drink appeared in a 1989 book called *The New American Bartender's Guide* by John Poister, yet the Jungle Bird remained obscure. This is no knock on that book, because let's remember, 1989 was well before the craft cocktail renaissance that we've been currently enjoying since 2000 or so.

Then tiki authority Jeff "Beachbum" Berry happened to encounter Poister's book in a bookstore bargain bin. He flipped through it and at first didn't see anything remarkable about the recipes—until one caught his eye. *Hmmm*, he thought, *a tiki-looking drink that has an apéritif bitter in it. That could be interesting!* So he bought the book. In 2002, Berry included the recipe in *Beachbum Berry's Intoxica*. As the decade wore on, more bartenders began discovering the drink, and before you knew it the Jungle Bird was becoming a darling of the craft cocktail scene.

I had my first Jungle Bird at a bar called Tweed in Stockholm, Sweden, in 2014. I somehow didn't know about the drink's growing fame, or my friend's role in discovering it. I still have the cocktail napkin on which I scribbled what I thought the recipe could be. I had showed it proudly to the Tweed bartender, who smiled and nodded, as if to say, "Yeah, that's pretty close!" I think you're going to love this drink.

recipe continues →

1½ ounces Jamaican dark rum
  (I like Appleton or Smith & Cross, but Angostura's new
  7-year-old is pretty amazing in this drink, too)

1½ ounces pineapple juice

¾ ounce Campari

½ ounce simple syrup (see page 6)

½ ounce fresh lime juice

1 pineapple wedge, for garnish

Combine the rum, pineapple juice, Campari, simple syrup, and lime juice in a cocktail shaker filled with ice and shake well. Strain into an Old-Fashioned glass filled with ice. Garnish with the pineapple wedge.

variation: Renowned bartender Shannon Mustipher, author of *Tiki: Modern Tropical Cocktails*, created an interesting take on the Jungle Bird called the Kingston Sound System. In addition to the aged Jamaican rum, she adds overproof rum and swaps out the Campari for the gentian-based liqueur Suze. It's really a great drink.

KNICKERBOCKER

This venerable old classic might just be one of the original Sour cocktails. It might also have been a harbinger of the tiki style of drinks, as much as eighty years before tiki was even a thing. With the juiced lime hull as garnish and the inclusion of orange curaçao and lime juice, it had "tiki" written all over it. Ahead of its time, this one was.

While the Knickerbocker was often referenced in the 1840s, it's not certain that all the references are about the same drink. After all, the term "Knickerbocker" was a popular nineteenth-century nickname for a New Yorker.

The earliest-known recipe is found in *The Bartender's Guide* (1862) by Jerry Thomas, and that is the recipe shown below.

makes 1 cocktail

2 ounces aged rum (Thomas called for a Santa Cruz rum, so a darker rum from somewhere other than Jamaica works)

½ ounce fresh lime juice or lemon juice

2 teaspoons raspberry syrup

½ teaspoon orange curaçao

1 lime or lemon hull, for garnish

Fresh berries in season, for garnish

Combine the rum, lime juice, raspberry syrup, and curaçao in a cocktail shaker filled with ice and shake well. Strain into a chilled cocktail glass and garnish with the lime hull and fresh berries.

LAST WORD

Every so often a forgotten classic not only gets rediscovered but also becomes the basis for bartenders to try their own riffs. We saw it happen with the Brooklyn Cocktail over the past twenty or so years, when bartenders (mostly in New York) created their own variations (often named for Brooklyn neighborhoods), starting with Vincenzo Errico's Red Hook, Julie Reiner's The Slope, Sam Ross's Cobble Hill, Chad Solomon's Bensonhurst, Joaquín Simo's Carroll Gardens, Audrey Saunders's Little Italy, Abby Gullo's Big Chief, and others. But since those aren't Sours, that's for another book. (*Psssst*, they're in my Manhattan book!)

The Last Word is another one of those rediscovered, riff-worthy drinks, to be sure. It's said to have been created in the years before Prohibition at the Detroit Athletic Club. In a contribution in *The Oxford Companion to Spirits and Cocktails*, St. John Frizell notes that it was mentioned in the Club's newsletter in 1916, and they wanted a whopping thirty-five cents for it! It fell into obscurity during Prohibition but was revived circa 2003 by Murray Stenson at the Zig Zag Café in Seattle. As an aside, I had the pleasure of enjoying a Last Word at the Detroit Athletic Club on a beautiful autumn day in 2022. The club's terrace overlooks Comerica Park, home of the Detroit Tigers baseball team.

What makes the Last Word distinctive is the unique flavor brought forth by green Chartreuse, an herbal liqueur made by the Carthusian monks in the Chartreuse Mountains of southeastern France. It's a blend of some 130 botanicals, and the recipe has remained a secret since 1605.

1 ounce London dry gin

1 ounce green Chartreuse

1 ounce fresh lime juice

1 ounce maraschino liqueur

Combine all the ingredients in a cocktail shaker filled with ice. Shake well, then strain into a chilled cocktail glass.

---

note: In recent times, there have been shortages of Chartreuse, reportedly because the Carthusian monks who produce this divine elixir were reluctant to increase production to meet rising demand. If shortages continue to plague the industry as you're reading this, you can turn to this list of other liqueurs to replace green Chartreuse in making this or any other drink (but of course, it won't be a true Last Word if you're using something else): Dolin Génépy, Faccia Brutto, Boomsma Claerkampster Clooster Bitter Liqueur, Ettaler Original Kloster Liqueur Grun, Bordiga Centum Herbis Liqueur, AngeVert (from Alpine Distilling), or Enrico Toro Centerba. In addition, one bartender recommended a 1:1 blend of Strega and Fernet-Branca.

recipe continues →

variations: Keeping with the Motor City theme, my friend Dave Kwiatkowski, of the Sugar House in Detroit's lively Corktown neighborhood, created his Famous Last Words there in 2015, containing equal parts Laphroaig single-malt Scotch, Bonal herbal liqueur, Aperol, and lemon juice. Perhaps, if you're way up in Northport, Michigan, he'll make you one at his new place, Fingers Crossed. Then there's the Final Ward, created in 2007 by Phil Ward at New York's legendary Death & Co. It contains equal parts rye, green Chartreuse, maraschino liqueur, and lemon juice. Or try Andrew Volk's Green Eyes, which has gin, green Chartreuse, and lime juice plus simple syrup and egg white. DiffordsGuide.com offers several other great options: the Closing Argument (mezcal, green Chartreuse, maraschino liqueur, lime juice), the Division Bell (mezcal, red Italian aperitivo, maraschino liqueur, and lime juice), the Dublin Minstrel (Irish whiskey, green Chartreuse, maraschino liqueur, and lime juice), the Dutch Word (genever oude, green Chartreuse, maraschino liqueur, and lime juice), the First Word (dry gin, maraschino liqueur, dry vermouth, lime juice, and an Italian red aperitivo), a Quiet Word (gold rum, green Chartreuse, maraschino liqueur, and lime juice), the Last Palabra (tequila, green Chartreuse, maraschino liqueur, lavender simple syrup, lime juice, and lavender bitters), the Latest Word (genever, green Chartreuse, maraschino liqueur, and lime juice), the Loose Talk (rye whiskey, Suze, yellow Chartreuse, lemon juice, lime juice, and Bénédictine), the Love & Murder (Campari, green Chartreuse, lime juice, simply syrup, and saline solution, invented by Nick Bennett at Porchlight in NYC), the Monte Cassino (rye whiskey, yellow Chartreuse, Bénédictine, and lemon juice), and the Neptune's Wrath (gin, absinthe, green Chartreuse, lemon juice, simple syrup, and egg white), and others. And, of course, see the Paper Plane (page 169); that modern classic is yet another Last Word riff.

LEATHERNECK

This tasty and simple little gem is credited to a man who's a wee bit of a hero to me. His name was Frank Farrell, and he led a *very* interesting life. Beginning in the late 1920s, he was a newspaper reporter and columnist operating out of Brooklyn, New York. Then, in 1939, he was one of the judges of the Miss America pageant (!), and that same year he worked as a special agent for the Office of Naval Intelligence. Later in the war, he joined the US Marine Corps and served as an intelligence officer, attached to the Office of Strategic Services (OSS), which was the predecessor of the Central Intelligence Agency. He had a brilliant career with the OSS, earning a Silver Star for his reconnaissance activities in the South Pacific (on Guadalcanal, New Georgia, and other posts), and broke up a postwar Nazi spy ring, resulting in the arrest of seven members of a German espionage network that was operating in China, despite Germany's surrender. From 1947 to 1967, he was a syndicated columnist for the *New York World-Telegram*, authoring the very popular "New York Day By Day" features column.

In 1951, a fellow by the name of Ted Saucier, who served as the publicist for the Waldorf-Astoria Hotel in New York City, published an iconic cocktail book called *Bottoms Up*. In addition to having about two hundred cocktail recipes (including the earliest-known recipe for the Last Word [see page 124]), it also was chock-full of rather risqué illustrations from twelve different artists and cartoonists. One of the drinks in Saucier's book was, you guessed it, the Leatherneck, one of many nicknames for a US Marine, along with gyrene, jarhead, devil dog, and others. (Trust me, I know—I've registered nearly eight hundred trademarks for the Marine Corps, including Leatherneck.) Frank wrote about the drink in his column on July 17, 1951, noting that he'd made this drink "to age overnight" his "new Marine major's gold leaves" (the rank insignia worn on his collar—apparently he'd recently been promoted while in the Marine Reserves), and that he'd "concocted" the drink "for Ted Saucier's forthcoming collection of favorite celeb grogs."

So it's pretty clear that Frank Farrell invented the Leatherneck, right? Well...remember that thing about success having many fathers? It seems that the Leatherneck was also featured twelve years earlier, in *The World Famous Cotton Club: 1939 Book of Mixed Drinks*, published by American Spirits, Inc., and compiled by Charlie Conolly, head bartender at the Players' Club. David Wondrich tipped me off to this seemingly conflicting claim. Did Farrell take credit for the Leatherneck eleven years after Harlem's iconic Cotton Club closed in 1940? Say it ain't so, Frank!

Maybe since Frank *was* a Manhattan-based society columnist in 1939 and had a degree of cachet already—and was therefore very likely to be a habitué of the Cotton Club (I mean, why wouldn't he be?)—he was tight enough with their bartender(s) to offer a drink creation to them. Further, according to a June 23, 1974, story in the *New York Times* (concerning the historic Greenwich Village nightclub Café Society), in 1939 Farrell "covered night clubs for the *World Telegram*." Maybe Farrell created the drink and offered it to Conolly, who added it to his book but neglected to credit its creator.

On that front, it's interesting to note that in the *Cotton Club* book, the Leatherneck is listed in the general category of "Cocktails," and *not* listed among "Cotton Club Specialty Cocktails," which you think it *would* be if invented there, no? Sigh, the world's full of mysteries . . . As for me, this is the story I'm going with: Farrell invented the Leatherneck in the late 1930s, and it first saw the light of day with Conolly's book in 1939, and then it resurfaced with Saucier's book and Frank's "New York Day By Day" column.

On a personal note, in 2019 I had the honor of presenting the Leatherneck at the annual William Donovan Award Dinner, held by the OSS Society in Washington, DC. I serve as toastmaster for OSS Society events, and on this evening, since former Secretary of Defense and Marine Corps General James "Chaos" Mattis was the recipient of the annual Donovan Award, I presented the Leatherneck cocktail as part of my toast, before a crowd of about eight hundred people. Sitting at my table that evening was Nina Farrell, Frank's daughter, who is as gracious as her dad was fascinating. As for Secretary Mattis (who apparently wasn't drinking that evening aside from the toast), he told me he was so intrigued by the drink that "it might make me fall off the wagon! In fact, it might make me want to *jump* off!" That little encounter with "Mad Dog" Mattis is among the highlights of my career as a toastmaster and would-be bartender!

Whoever invented the drink (I still believe it was Farrell), here's how to make it.

makes 1 cocktail

2 ounces blended whiskey (such as a Canadian whisky, or use a good rye)

¾ ounce blue curaçao (see Note)

½ ounce fresh lime juice

1 lime wheel, for garnish

Combine the whiskey, curaçao, and lime juice in a cocktail shaker filled with ice and shake well. Strain into a chilled cocktail glass and garnish with the lime wheel. Or do as Frank (and Ted) suggested: "Shake violently on the rocks and serve in a cocktail glass. . . . Stop smoking. Fasten your seat-belts. Empty your fountain pens. Because after two gulps, you'll seriously consider yourself capable of straightening out Chinese fire drills." Whatever the heck that means!

---

note: Blue curaçao is nothing more than orange curaçao with blue food dye added. As such, don't rush out to buy blue when you have orange (or Cointreau or any good triple sec). Just add a drop or two of blue food coloring.

LION OF BALTIMORE

During the War of 1812, the US didn't have much of a navy. As a result, in the fight against the vastly superior British Royal Navy, the US military often had to supplement its capabilities with "privateers." These were privately owned vessels, manned by volunteers—or mercenaries, if you will. One such sailing ship was the *Lion of Baltimore*. During the British Royal Navy's Maryland campaign in the summer of 1814, which resulted in the burning of the US Capitol and the White House, the *Lion* wreaked havoc on British ships in the upper Chesapeake Bay. As British forces then turned their attention northward toward Baltimore, where they'd eventually bombard Fort McHenry (you know, the whole "Star-Spangled Banner" story), the *Lion*'s crew knew they were outnumbered. They tried to hide the ship in the waters of nearby Bodkin Creek, to "live to fight another day." Unfortunately, the Brits discovered the *Lion* and burned her to the waterline. To this day archaeologists are trying to locate the *Lion*'s remains at the bottom of Bodkin Creek or the adjacent Chesapeake Bay.

The British were defeated by the American forces and failed to capture either Fort McHenry or Baltimore. Indeed, in the battle around nearby Sparrow's Point, Maryland sharpshooters killed the British commander, General Ross. His body was loaded into a cask of Jamaican rum to preserve it for the long voyage to Nova Scotia, where he would be buried.

Ever since 2003, I've kept a sailboat at our family's vacation home on Bodkin Creek, and one day in 2013, my dad and I went for a sail on Chesapeake Bay. We accomplished a feat that we were only able to do a handful of times together: We sailed from about two miles out in the Bay, through the channel, and all the way up Main Creek and into our slip, entirely "under sail," meaning we didn't rely one bit on the boat's engine. Deeming that to be worthy of a celebratory cocktail, I set about making us something special.

I told my dad the story of the *Lion of Baltimore*. I started off making what I originally intended would be just a simple rum Manhattan, using Jamaican rum to honor the *Lion*, General Ross, and the valor of the Maryland sharpshooters.

But then I thought I'd add a little lime juice to brighten it up, then some of the delectable pimento bitters that my good friend Dale DeGroff had recently released. It needed a bit of sweetening, so I added just a touch of orgeat. I'm happy to say that the drink has developed a little bit of a following; in fact, Dale saw fit to include it in his essential *The New Craft of the Cocktail* (2020). I hope you'll like it. My dad and I certainly did.

makes 1 cocktail

2 ounces Jamaican dark rum (such as Smith & Cross or Appleton)

1 ounce sweet vermouth (Dolin or Martini work well)

¾ ounce fresh lime juice

¼ ounce orgeat

2 or 3 dashes Dale DeGroff's pimento bitters

Combine all the ingredients in a cocktail shaker filled with ice. Shake well and strain into a chilled cocktail glass.

A LITTLE DEATH

It was summer of 2022, and my wife, our daughter Madeleine, and I were driving cross-country from Northern Michigan en route to the Yellowstone area of Montana and Wyoming. Our plan was to stop for the night in Bismarck, North Dakota. I was behind the wheel, and somewhere in Minnesota I said to Maddie, "Do me a favor, take my phone and go to Facebook and post this for me: 'Seeking food and drink options in Bismarck, ND.'" She looked at me with her classic side-eye: "Seriously?" I replied, "You never know." Within the hour, bartending great Kate Gerwin, who'd previously lived and worked in Bismarck, gave us a great dinner recommendation and suggested that we "hit up Thomas & Moriarty's for drinks. Michael Kashey will certainly be there to entertain you." We went there for a nightcap and didn't want to leave.

Michael is a native of North Dakota who spent seven years in Germany (five with the US Army), then came back to Bismarck and co-opened Thomas & Moriarty's in 2018. When I told him about this book, he offered this little gem of a drink, and it's become a favorite. As he explained:

> While planning the inaugural menu for Thomas & Moriarty's, we knew we wanted to have a drink named after the old literary term for an orgasm, "a little death." The drink itself was first made in the unfinished venue on a metal prep table acting as a bar well, with a large paint bucket as a dump sink, all under the light of one single construction light. This simple drink was nailed the first time and we knew that was our Little Death. Since then it has become our most iconic cocktail, and its fall variation, La Petite Mort, boasts a richer profile.

makes 1 cocktail

1½ ounces sloe gin (Hayman's or Sipsmith)

¾ ounce fresh lemon juice

¼ ounce simple syrup (see page 6)

½ ounce apricot liqueur (Rothman & Winter or Luxardo)

1 to 2 ounces chilled Prosecco or other sparkling wine

1 lemon twist, for garnish

Combine the gin, lemon juice, simple syrup, and apricot liqueur in a cocktail shaker filled with ice. Shake well and strain into a highball glass filled with ice. Top with the Prosecco, then garnish with the lemon twist.

variation: For the "winter version," simply substitute a good fig puree for the apricot liqueur.

the drinks **133**

MADISON AVENUE

This delicious drink was created in 1936 by Eddie Woelke (see page 105), after he'd returned to New York City from Havana after the end of Prohibition. He would serve until 1941 as "the Weylin Hotel's chief drink dispenser," as noted in the *Brooklyn Daily Eagle* on October 2, 1936. It seems that Eddie entered, and won, a cocktail competition held at his old stomping grounds, the Hotel Biltmore, as part of "Madison Avenue Week," which celebrated the 100th anniversary of that street.

Another newspaper story also heralded the drink competition, but focused on a tempest in a teapot in the bartending world at the time. The event coincided with the annual meeting of the International Barmen Association. The headline of the October 13, 1936, story in the *Wilkes-Barre Evening News* fairly screamed out "BARTENDERS OF WORLD AGAINST ALL BAR MAIDS," with the subheadline "Also Would Exclude Women Patrons from Standing or SITTING AT BARS." Indeed, "a ban on women on either side of a 'bar' in the interests of temperate drinking was urged today by bartenders" of that association. "The organization is not only unalterably opposed to women drinking at bars but it is even more concerned with the growing tendency to replace the bartender with the barmaid." Oh my!

And why, pray tell, did this august group of mansplainers, er, I mean barmen, feel this way? Association president Louis Wolff explained: "Liquor alone can cause enough trouble, why add women? When you get a pretty miss behind the bar you invite trouble . . . Barmaids are not in keeping with the aim of the liquor industry—moderation in drinking. It all boils down to the age-old tendency [of] women—they flirt . . . So, put a ban on them, we say."

Did Wolff call for a complete ban? No, "women patrons should be served their alcoholic beverages seated at tables and not with one foot against the bar rail. The powder puff and the lipstick curb free speech, they say, and only can lead to a deterioration of the art of drinking." *OH. MY. GOD.*

There are plenty of other examples of discrimination against women in the so-called hospitality industry. But let's instead talk about how to make that Madison Avenue cocktail, shall we? It's really delicious. The recipe is a slightly modified version from the news story.

1½ ounces white rum

¾ ounce fresh lime juice

⅓ ounce Cointreau

3 mint sprigs

1 lime wheel, for garnish

Combine the rum, lime juice, Cointreau, and 2 mint sprigs in a shaker and muddle the mint. Add ice and shake well, then strain into a chilled cocktail glass. Garnish with the lime wheel and remaining sprig of mint.

variation: Similar to how a Daiquiri can be extended into a Mojito, add more mint and soda water, then serve it on the rocks. You'll end up with a great summertime refresher.

MAIN STAGE

New Orleans is something of an adopted hometown for me, and my wife and I visit whenever we can. It's one of those towns where you literally plan your day around where you're going to eat and drink. Among our favorite restaurants in recent years is Lillette on Magazine Street in Uptown. Their cocktail menu offers a delicious drink that, like the Bramble (page 51) and New York Sour (see page 231), has a finishing touch that's a delight to behold. It was created by bartender Anna Gillcrist, who offers her own comments on the drink:

> The Main Stage cocktail is what I would describe as a Tequila Sour with a bitter finish. Several years ago while working at a former mixology bar in Los Angeles, a happy accident occurred when I added Campari to a gin cocktail about three steps too late. I watched as the bright red apéritif slid down the inside of the glass, setting itself beautifully at the bottom, creating a two-toned cocktail. While coming up with new beverage ideas for Lillet in 2022, I remembered this trick and put it together with the spirit that forever has my heart, tequila. Patrons have the option of mixing the drink together from the start, or sipping it as is, tasting the sweet and the sour before being hit with that familiarly delicious and bitter Campari taste we know and love. We decided on the name "Main Stage" because I came up with the cocktail right before the New Orleans Jazz & Heritage Festival. We wanted some of the cocktail names to have a musical theme!

1½ ounces reposado tequila

½ ounce Domaine de Canton ginger liqueur

¾ ounce fresh grapefruit juice

½ ounce fresh lime juice

¼ ounce simple syrup (see page 6)

¼ ounce Campari, as a sink (see page 5)

1 lime peel, for garnish

Combine the tequila, ginger liqueur, grapefruit juice, lime juice, and simple syrup in a cocktail shaker filled with ice and shake well. Strain into an Old-Fashioned glass with 1 giant ice cube inside. Gently pour the Campari down the side of the glass as a sink and garnish with the lime peel.

MAI TAI

This is perhaps the most celebrated—and most often poorly made—of the entire canon of tiki drinks. Similar to the "daiquiri" and "martini" you might see on certain menus, you just don't know what you're going to get, as authenticity often isn't held in high esteem when those terms are being bandied about. Indeed, if you order a Mai Tai in some random bar, the only thing you can guarantee is that it'll have rum, something that resembles tropical fruit juice, and probably an umbrella. I actually went to a poolside bar in San Diego back in 2014, and there was a sign on the bar that said, "WE'RE PROUD TO SAY THAT OUR MAI-TAI CONTAINS ZERO FRUIT JUICE!" But when the drink is made correctly, it's sublime. And that's what you'll find in the recipe shown below.

Cocktail lore tells us that Victor "Trader Vic" Bergeron created the drink on a whim one day, and he wrote about it in his *Revised Bar Guide* in 1944:

> I was at my service bar in my Oakland restaurant. I took down a bottle of seventeen-year-old rum. It was J. Wray [&] Nephew from Jamaica; surprisingly golden in color, medium bodied, but with the rich pungent flavor particular to the Jamaican blends. The flavor of this great rum wasn't meant to be overpowered with heavy additions of fruit juices and flavorings. I took a fresh lime, added some orange curaçao from Holland, a dash of rock candy syrup, and a dollop of French orgeat, for its subtle almond flavor. A generous amount of shaved ice and vigorous shaking by hand produced the marriage I was after. Half the lime shell went in for color, [and] I stuck in a branch of fresh mint.

He said he first served the drink to friends, a couple visiting from Tahiti named Ham and Carrie Guild. Carrie smiled and said, "Mai tai roa ae," which means "the best" or "awesome" in Tahitian. And so the drink was named.

In his excellent book *Potions of the Caribbean*, Jeff "Beachbum" Berry noted that Vic was fond of telling folks that "anybody who says I didn't create this drink is a dirty stinker." Now, who would say such a thing? Donn Beach, that's who. Beach maintained that Vic based the Mai Tai on one of Beach's creations: "The Q.B. Cooler was the basis for a drink he took with him, and he called it the Mai Tai." But Fred Fung, a longtime assistant to Vic, disagreed. While it was true that Vic copied the whole Don the Beachcomber vibe when he founded Trader Vic's, it wasn't the case with the drink. Fung said, "But the Mai Tai, he did concoct that, and Carrie Guild did name it." Then again, as Beachbum points out, isn't the Mai Tai awfully similar to Constante Ribalaigua's Golden Glove, which is the same drink but without orgeat? Hmm . . . As I keep saying in this book, success has many fathers.

makes 1 cocktail

2 ounces dark rum (Berry recommends a 1:1 blend of Jamaican rum and rhum agricole vieux)

1 ounce fresh lime juice

½ ounce orange curaçao

½ ounce orgeat

¼ ounce simple syrup (see page 6)

1 mint sprig, for garnish

1 lime hull, for garnish

Combine the rum, lime juice, curaçao, orgeat, and simple syrup in a cocktail shaker filled with crushed ice and shake well. Transfer the contents of the shaker (ice and all) to an Old-Fashioned glass and garnish with the mint sprig and lime hull.

variation: The 1939 El Floridita cocktail booklet (see page 75) featured Constante's Golden Glove, which contained 2 ounces white rum, 1 teaspoon each of Cointreau and sugar, and ½ ounce fresh lime juice, mixed in a blender and garnished with an orange peel.

MARGARITA

It's interesting that two of the most popular cocktails in the world, the Margarita and the Daiquiri (page 75)—both of them Sours—have not only survived but thrived through the Dark Ages of bartending. Back in the 1970s and 1980s, when frozen drinks were all the rage, both of these classics were being made so badly, but we lapped them up anyway with great zeal. The Daiquiri was nothing more than an alcoholic slushie, and the Margarita was made with crappy "mixto" tequila (I'll explain momentarily), bottom-shelf triple sec, and artificial lime juice and/or sour mix. Now that there are better tequilas and awareness about how tequila should be made, and a commitment (from most places, anyway) to fresh juices, the Margarita can be a sublime and refreshing cocktail. That said, you can still get a bad Margarita. (Be wary of what they might call a "Skinny Margarita," which will likely be an overly sweet, artificial drink.)

Okay, what do I mean by "mixto"? Think of tequila like a crab cake or lobster roll. Wouldn't you want it to be made from 100% crab or lobster—not with breadcrumbs, cheaper fish parts, and other fillers? A "mixto" tequila is a tequila that isn't made from 100% blue agave—it might contain only 51 percent blue agave and the rest "neutral spirit." Read the label!

As is the case with so, so many classic drinks, we don't have a firm fix on who invented it, or where. While there are competing stories about the first drink to be made with tequila, lime, and triple sec, the earliest-known reference to the drink by name is from a September 1953 newspaper in California, in which a columnist spoke of encountering a Margarita (complete with the salted rim!) in Ensenada, Mexico.

Being a teenager in the 1970s, my first exposure to the drink was not in liquid form; it was on the radio. The late, great Jimmy Buffett's song "Margaritaville" was blowing up in the summer of 1977, when I was a rising junior in high school, champing at the bit to turn sixteen and get my driver's license.

Coarse salt, for rimming the glass

Lime wedge

2 ounces 100% blue agave blanco tequila

½ ounce Cointreau or Ferrand dry curaçao

¾ ounce fresh lime juice

Pour about 1 tablespoon of coarse salt onto a small dish. Moisten the rim of a chilled margarita glass with the lime wedge, then dip the rim in the salt to coat. Set the glass and the lime wedge aside. Combine the tequila, Cointreau, and lime juice in a cocktail shaker filled with ice and shake well. Strain into the prepared glass and garnish with the lime wedge.

variations: If you want the drink on the rocks, either transfer it directly from the shaker to the glass or strain it into the glass over ice. For a frozen Margarita, blend the drink with crushed ice. Use agave syrup in place of the triple sec and make it a Tommy's Margarita, invented in 1990 by Julio Bermejo at Tommy's Mexican Restaurant in San Francisco. Or make a Cadillac Margarita by using Grand Marnier instead of triple sec. Or try the Bottlerocket, invented by Theo Lieberman at Milk & Honey. It features blanco tequila, lime juice, honey syrup, jalapeño, and soda water. I've used Domaine de Canton ginger liqueur in place of triple sec with great success to make a Margarita de Canton. Also, similar to the Tommy's Margarita, using honey syrup (see page 7) as the sweetener renders a delicious Tequila Honeysuckle. How about a Margarita made with aged (*reposado*) tequila? That'd be a Repo Margarita. And if you *really* want to give your mouth a flavor sensation, try the Jägerita, basically a Margarita made with Jägermeister in place of the tequila. You knew Jäger wasn't just made for shots!

MARY PICKFORD

I know the term gets thrown about a lot lately, but to me, Mary Pickford was one of Hollywood's original badasses. Known as "America's Sweetheart," "the girl with the curls," and "the Biograph girl," Pickford was one of the motion picture industry's earliest stars, and a major force both in front of and behind the camera. In 1919, she cofounded United Artists, along with her husband, Douglas Fairbanks (see page 81); Charlie Chaplin (see page 59); and D. W. Griffith. She was one of Hollywood's most successful actors, winning an Academy Award for her first sound picture, *Coquette*, and was awarded an honorary Oscar for her contributions to the industry in 1976. One of the first advocates of film preservation, Pickford was one of the founders of the Academy of Motion Picture Arts and Sciences and was enormously active in philanthropy.

And, it seems, she was huge in Cuba, as was her husband, Douglas Fairbanks. But did they both travel to Havana together, as it might seem? This is from MaryPickford.org, the official website of the Mary Pickford Foundation:

> The most oft-repeated story is that the Mary Pickford cocktail was "invented" in Cuba in the '20s in honor of the silent-screen star, who was visiting the island along with her husband Douglas Fairbanks while they were making a movie there. Sometimes in the telling, they are accompanied by Charlie Chaplin. It's a nice yarn, but a review of Mary and Doug's schedule reveals no trips to Cuba—and they never made a film there during their marriage. What's more, Chaplin . . . rarely, if ever, traveled with them. When Pickford was at Independent Moving Pictures in the early 1910s, along with her then husband Owen Moore, they did make several films in Cuba. However, Mary was miserable there for quite a few reasons, including the humid climate that wreaked havoc on her fabled curls.

As for when the drink was invented, Jeff Berry's entry in *The Oxford Companion to Spirits and Cocktails* notes that "newspaper accounts confirm that she vacationed there in 1922, when Kaufman most likely invented his drink," and it was so popular at El Floridita (see page 75) during and after Prohibition that Costante Ribalaigua could often be seen "making six at a time."

Oddly enough, and similar to the Douglas Fairbanks, there seems to be some variance in the drink, even at the same bar! The *Sloppy Joe's* booklet for the 1931–32 season has the Mary Pickford being made with equal parts rum, pineapple juice, and Noilly Prat dry vermouth, with "drops" of grenadine and orange curaçao added. Here, just as I did with the Fairbanks, I'm offering the most recent of the *Sloppy Joe's* recipes (from 1936), which is shown below. Hollywood, and Havana, are full of mysteries, it seems.

makes 1 cocktail

1½ ounces light rum

1½ ounces pineapple juice

1 teaspoon grenadine

1 teaspoon maraschino liqueur

Combine all the ingredients in a cocktail shaker filled with ice. Shake well and strain into a chilled cocktail glass.

MEXICAN "FIRING SQUAD" SPECIAL

This delicious drink made its debut in Charles H. Baker Jr.'s 1939 book *The Gentleman's Companion*. Baker had an inimitable style to his writing. As for this drink, Baker noted that it "IS A CREATION WE ALMOST BECAME WRECKED upon in—of ALL SPOTS—LA CUCURACHA [*sic*] Bar in MEXICO CITY, in 1937." Even his use of all caps was entertaining. If you don't know much about Baker, he and his intrepid (and stinking rich) wife, Pauline Paulsen, traveled the world on their sailing yacht, the *Marmion*, gathering food and drink recipes, and he published them in his various *Companions*, referenced herein, as well as in *Esquire*. Occasionally Baker and his wife would break free from local guidance and find a great drink, such as this one. Per Baker, La Cucaracha was "where an aristocrat native oughtn't to be seen!"

makes 1 cocktail

2 ounces tequila

¾ ounce fresh lime juice

⅓ to ½ ounce grenadine (depending on how sweet you want it)

2 dashes Angostura bitters

1 orange slice, for garnish

1 pineapple wedge, for garnish

1 cocktail cherry, for garnish

Combine the tequila, lime juice, grenadine, and bitters in a cocktail shaker filled with ice and shake well. Strain into an Old-Fashioned glass filled with ice and garnish with the orange slice, pineapple wedge, and cherry.

MEXICAN
RAZOR BLADE

My good mate Jason Crawley created this drink for the bar Fortunate Son, located in the Newtown section of Sydney, Australia. The bar won Australia's "Bar of the Year" award in 2022, and I have no doubt that this drink is part of their success. Jason tells me that the drink "sells like hot-pancakes as it turns your face inside out in the best possible way."

Crawley's an Englishman by birth who moved to Oz in 2000. Mind you, a great many Brits made that voyage to the land down under back in the nineteenth century; however, they were compelled to make the trip for other reasons, notably *prison*. I'd like to think that Jason's motives for the move were completely different.

Seriously, Crawley is an internationally recognized figure in the world's drinks community, and in 2018 he was awarded the "Outstanding Contribution Award" for his efforts by *Australian Bartender* magazine at their annual Australian Bar Awards. Further, his amazing Imperial Shaker, which you have to see to believe, was inducted into the Museum of the American Cocktail in New Orleans, and the shaker is in use in over sixty countries around the world. Crawley is also the head of Crawley's Bartender Syrups, which are quite popular in the bar-and-restaurant scene in China, Australia, New Zealand, and the Asia Pacific region. Not only is Crawley's grenadine used at Raffles Hotel in their Singapore Sling (see page 206), but the drink itself is made in Crawley's custom "Sling Shaker."

This is a lovely drink, and like the Jungle Bird (page 121) and Main Stage (page 136), it's nice to see Campari playing a supporting role in a great cocktail. Cheers, mate!

recipe continues →

1½ ounces silver tequila

1 ounce white grapefruit juice

½ ounce fresh lime juice

½ ounce Campari

½ ounce simple syrup (see page 6)

3 to 5 drops brine from Golden State hot chile peppers (or use a favorite hot sauce of your own)

1 medium egg white

Jason does the dry shake (see page 4) thing a bit differently; he does it *after* shaking the drink with ice. Here's how: Combine the tequila, grapefruit juice, lime juice, Campari, simple syrup, and chile brine in a cocktail shaker filled with ice and shake well. Remove the ice from the shaker, add the egg white, and shake again for about 15 seconds. Strain the drink into a chilled cocktail glass.

MIDORI SOUR

If you're looking for a drink that best represents all of the excesses of the 1970s—the era of disco music and flashy, statusy nightclubs, with people dressed in *Saturday Night Fever* attire; the men sporting huge porn-staches, giant collars on their open-necked shirts, gold chains, bellbottom slacks and platform shoes; the women with their Farrah hair and slinky dresses and octagonal eyewear—the Midori Sour might just be this drink. After all, it made its stateside debut at Studio 54, that iconic Manhattan disco.

Midori was launched in the 1970s by Japanese company Suntory, known better for its beer and whiskies, and was marketed heavily in the latter part of the decade. Ads encouraged folks to try it as an after-dinner drink, or in cocktails such as the Universe (a first-prize winner in the 1978 US Bartenders Guild Competition), the Melancholy Baby, the Melon Margarita, and of course the Midori Sour. According to an article in Liquor.com, "Midori's flavor is derived from Japanese muskmelons and the cantaloupe-like yubari fruit, which are both infused into neutral grain spirits. Before bottling, the melon spirit is blended with brandy and sugar and dosed with food coloring to achieve its characteristic bright-green color." Ah, food coloring . . . As a kid in the 1970s I remember everyone freaking out over Red No. 2. (Don't eat those red M&M's!)

This is a drink that, similar to the Gimlet (page 99) can be made well if you make it with fresh ingredients (freshly squeezed lime juice and lemon juice, not Rose's or the artificially flavored and sweetened Sour mix they were probably slinging at "the 54"). So, if you're nostalgic for that era, maybe fix a Midori Sour, put on your disco garb, and listen to "Le Freak" by Chic. You know, "just come on down to the 54, find your spot out on the floor, *ahh* FREAK OUT!" Just don't freak out about the food coloring.

recipe continues →

1 ounce vodka

1 ounce Midori

½ ounce fresh lemon juice

½ ounce fresh lime juice

2 to 4 ounces soda water, to top

1 lemon or lime wheel, for garnish

Combine the vodka, Midori, lemon juice, and lime juice in a cocktail shaker filled with ice and shake well. Strain into a Collins glass filled with ice. Add the soda water to the shaker to chill it and release the flavor clinging to the ice, then strain it into the drink. Stir well, then garnish with the lemon or lime wheel.

MISSIONARY'S DOWNFALL

In *The Oxford Companion to Spirits and Cocktails*, tiki authority Jeff "Beachbum" Berry describes the creator of this drink, Ernest Raymond Beaumont Gantt (who later changed his name to Donn Beach and open the historic "Don the Beachcomber" chain), as "a mixologist and restaurateur who almost single-handedly created the post-Prohibition 'tiki drink' category."

When Gantt was eighteen, his father gave him a choice: Here's some money; go to college or travel the world. Gantt chose the latter and over the next several years was a bit of a vagabond. He ended up in Los Angeles, and in 1934 opened a place called Don's Beachcomber (later known as Don the Beachcomber), a bar and restaurant with a South Seas theme. It had a menu full of what he called "Rhum Rhapsodies," rum-based drinks flavored with various fruit juices and obscure liqueurs. One of those "Rhapsodies" was the Missionary's Downfall. The name was intended to have a little fun with the idea of pious (and teetotaling) missionaries venturing to the tropics to convert the pagan heathens to Christianity and succumbing to pleasures of the flesh.

makes 1 cocktail

15 mint leaves, plus 1 mint sprig for garnish

1 ounce gold rum

½ ounce peach schnapps, peach liqueur, or peach syrup

½ ounce pineapple juice

½ ounce fresh lime juice

⅓ ounce honey syrup (3:1 water to honey)

Combine the mint leaves and rum in a cocktail shaker and muddle the mint well. Add ice to the shaker, then add the schnapps, pineapple juice, lime juice, and honey syrup and shake well. Strain into a Collins glass filled with crushed ice and garnish with the mint sprig.

MISS SAIGON

This delicious drink comes from my old pal Jo-Jo Valenzuela, one of Washington, DC's best bartenders and owner of two adjoining bars in the District's Adams Morgan neighborhood: Tiki on 18th and the Game. Jo-Jo and I both lay claim to be the world's best at parallel parking, and one of these days we'll have to go mano a mano to determine the undisputed champ. In the meantime, here's Jo-Jo's offering:

> I needed to come up with ideas for a Vietnamese cocktail bar that I was consulting on. I wanted to create a purple cocktail. Butterfly pea flower was obviously the first ingredient that came to mind, and the drink's name came in second. For the name I chose "Miss Saigon," named after the former name of the most populous city in Vietnam, and the 1904 opera, *Madama Butterfly*. I unintentionally crossed a Pisco Sour [page 182] with an Aviation [page 36; also the Bloomfield, page 50]. For the garnish, I wanted a little red color on top, and possibly add a flavor common in Vietnamese cuisine, that being anise. Peychaud's bitters, known for its red color and licorice flavor, completed the artwork. The final product is a visually stunning, refreshing cocktail, with complex floral notes and a beautiful mouthfeel.

2 ounces pisco

¼ ounce crème de violette

¾ ounce Butterfly Pea Flower Syrup (recipe follows)

1 ounce egg white

¾ ounce fresh lime juice

Peychaud's bitters, for garnish

Pansy blossoms, for garnish

Combine the pisco, crème de violette, butterfly pea flower syrup, egg white, and lime juice in cocktail shaker with 1 large ice cube. Shake well for about 15 seconds, then remove the ice cube and dry shake (see page 4) for 15 seconds. Strain into a chilled cocktail glass, then garnish with a few splashes of Peychaud's bitters and a couple of pansy blossoms.

BUTTERFLY PEA FLOWER SYRUP   *makes 2 cups*

20 grams (4 teaspoons) butterfly pea flower petals

1 cup sugar

In a small saucepan, combine the butterfly pea flower petals, sugar, and 1 cup water and bring to a simmer over medium-low heat, stirring well until the sugar has dissolved and the petals have had a chance to steep. Let cool for at least 3 hours, then strain the syrup into a clean container. Cover and store in the refrigerator. It will keep for up to 7 days.

MONARCH

I discovered this little gem at one of our favorite local restaurants, Buck's Fishing & Camping. Buck's has been a DC institution since 2003, and was enshrined in *Washington Post* food critic Tom Sietsema's "DC Restaurant Hall of Fame" as "the place to go when you want something familiar and fabulous." This drink certainly checks both boxes. It was invented in April 2023 by bartender Evan Peters, who tells me he created the cocktail to pay tribute to his favorite early summer drink, the Gimlet (page 99). As Peters says,

> This classic Gimlet kicks off with the acidic fresh lime juice the moment your lips touch the glass, quickly melting into a refreshing botanical bouquet from your gin of choice. Colleagues had predicted that mezcal would be the spirit of the summer. Further, our general manager Cortney Jackson had been telling me about her new cocktail ingredient obsession: butterfly pea flower extract. With these inspirations, I think I've created an easily made cocktail with a deceptively complex flavor profile and striking presentation. With a split base of gin and mezcal, you're getting dueling notes of smoky fried banana, pineapple, and citrus from the Banhez mezcal and a well-balanced, floral blend of juniper, lemon zest, and cinnamon via the gin. Of course, the pea flower extract makes the cocktail truly sing, contributing subtle floral and herbal notes and adding a depth that highlights the floral gin and nutty, fruity wood-fired mezcal.

As for the name, it was also a collaboration with Cortney, "Monarch" as a reference to the butterfly pea flower extract as well as the notion of feeling like royalty when enjoying the drink. It's a great cocktail, and it's nice to know I can enjoy one within walking distance!

2 or 3 drops butterfly pea flower extract (Evan uses Wild Hibiscus Flower
   Company's B'lure flower extract)

1 Luxardo gourmet cocktail cherry, for garnish

1 ounce fresh lime juice

1 ounce simple syrup (see page 6)

1½ ounces Botanist Islay dry gin

½ ounce Banhez Espadin & Barril mezcal

1 edible flower, for garnish (optional)

Place the pea flower extract and the cherry in a chilled Nick & Nora glass, then set
aside. Combine the lime juice, simple syrup, gin, and mezcal in a cocktail shaker
filled with ice and shake well. Strain into the prepared glass and garnish with the
edible flower, if desired.

MOJITO

Believed to have been invented in Cuba in the early part of the twentieth century, the Mojito has enjoyed a renaissance that began in the 1990s and continues today. It's basically a Rum Collins with mint, and it is as refreshing as the day is long. The earliest-known appearance of the drink came in the 1929 book *Libro de Cocktail* by Juan A. Lasa, where it went by the name Mojo de Ron (*ron* being the Spanish word for "rum"). It appeared as the Mojito in the 1931–32 season cocktail menu booklet from Sloppy Joe's Bar in Havana.

The drink is commonly (and erroneously) identified as among the favorite drinks of American novelist Ernest Hemingway, on whose drink preferences I've written a book. There is a bar in Havana called La Bodeguita del Medio with a handwritten sign on the wall that reads, "My mojito in La Bodeguita My Daiquiri in El Floridita," and it's signed "Ernest Hemingway." It sure looks like his handwriting. Well, it *should*! See, as author Tom Miller explains in his 2008 book titled *Trading with the Enemy: A Yankee Travels Through Castro's Cuba*, a friend of Hemingway's, Fernando Campoamor, was doing some public relations work for the fledgling La Bodeguita, which wanted more bar business. So he hired a graphic artist who used Hemingway handwriting samples provided by Campoamor to create the bogus sign. Business has been brisk for well over sixty years due to this bit of savvy marketing (if you're being sympathetic) or outright forgery (if not).

Hemingway tended to write about what he drank, in letters and in his fiction. And he never once mentioned either the Mojito or La Bodeguita. And, with concerns about diabetes (see the Daiquiri, page 75), he likely couldn't tolerate such a sweet drink. But what're you gonna do? You can't prove a negative, right?

The traditional way to make the drink is to muddle the mint along with the rum, simple syrup, and lime juice, then add ice and soda water, and stir. I make my Mojito a bit differently from others. I don't muddle the mint, since I think it does nothing but clog up your straw. And I think you'll get more flavor from the lime if you shake it. So, I shake the drink with the mint (and everything else but the soda water) in the shaker and filter out most of the mint when I strain it. And it's not like I'm the only one out there adding mint to the shaker. In her classic Old Cuban, Audrey Saunders does the same thing (see the variations).

To make it my way, follow this recipe.

makes 1 cocktail

2 ounces light rum

½ ounce simple syrup (see page 6)

½ ounce fresh lime juice

6 to 8 mint leaves, plus 1 mint sprig for garnish

4 ounces soda water, for topping the drink

1 lime wheel, for garnish

Combine the rum, simple syrup, lime juice, and mint leaves in a cocktail shaker filled with ice. Shake well, then strain into a Collins glass filled with ice. Rinse the shaker (see page 5) with the soda water, then strain the soda into the glass. Garnish with the lime wheel and mint sprig.

variations: Use an aged (6- to 10-year) rum or Champagne or other sparkling wine in place of the soda water, add a couple dashes of Angostura bitters, and serve it up in a chilled cocktail glass—that's Audrey Saunders's delicious Old Cuban, which she invented circa 2001 when working at a Midtown Manhattan restaurant called Beacon. The Madison Avenue (page 134) has a similar vibe, but it's made with gin. Or something of a mash-up between the New York Sour (see page 231) and Mojito would be the JFK Harris, invented by Zachary Gelnaw-Rubin at Milk & Honey in the 2000s. It's basically a Mojito but with lemon juice (not lime) and a splash of red wine at the finish.

MOSCOW MULE

Whether a craft cocktail geek wants to admit it or not, in terms of popularity, vodka is the world's number one spirit. As a baby boomer, and having grown up in an era of flavorless white bread, iceberg lettuce, and (until the craft beer boom that thankfully began in the 1980s) bland beer, it's yet another reminder that a vast majority of folks still want the "lowest common denominator" when it comes to food and drink. But circa 1940, vodka was barely on the radars of bartenders and drinkers. Then along came the Moscow Mule and the Bloody Mary. I guess you could say that both drinks were the "early adopters" of vodka as the base ingredient in a mixed drink.

According to cocktail folklore, the Moscow Mule was created one evening at a bar called the Cock'n Bull in Los Angeles. It seems that John Martin, an executive with Heublein (the American importer/promoter of Smirnoff, pretty much the industry leader of the day), and Jack Morgan, owner of the bar. Both gents had excess merchandise they had to unload—Martin the vodka, and Morgan his own house brand of ginger beer. "Dadgummit," the men said to each other, "if we could only figure out how to move this stuff! Maybe if we invented a drink . . ." And the rest is bartending history. There are a few variations on this tale, but you get the drift. The drink was (and still is) served in a copper mug (and you can still find collectible mugs from the Cock'n Bull on eBay and other auction sites).

However it went down, the Moscow Mule became one of the most popular vodka drinks through the 1940s and '50s, and just as it was starting to fade in popularity, Smirnoff revived the drink in the early '60s, calling it the Smirnoff Mule. If you want to have some fun, check out their magazine ads online, featuring the likes of Woody Allen, Groucho Marx, and other celebs.

2 ounces vodka

½ ounce fresh lime juice

3 to 4 ounces ginger beer

Combine all the ingredients in a copper mug or highball glass filled with ice. Stir and serve.

variations: As noted on page 27, there's not a lot of difference between the categories of Mule and Buck. Here are a few classic variations on the theme, all made with the same proportions as the Moscow Mule. There's the Gin Buck (gin, lemon or lime juice, ginger ale), the Bourbon (or Kentucky) Buck (bourbon, lemon or lime juice, ginger ale), Applejack Buck (applejack/apple brandy, lemon or lime juice, ginger ale), Brandy Buck (brandy, lemon or lime juice, ginger ale), the Mamie Taylor (Scotch, lemon juice, ginger ale), Dark 'n' Stormy (Gosling's Black Seal Rum, lime juice, ginger beer), and El Diablo (white rum, equal parts crème de cassis and lime juice, ginger ale). In the *Trader Vic Bartender's Guide*, Victor Bergeron offered the Mexican El Diablo (tequila, equal parts crème de cassis and lime juice, and ginger ale). If you want to stick with vodka as the spirit, try the Palma Fizz, invented by Sasha Petraske; it's a Moscow Mule with a few drops of rose water added as a finishing touch. Then you have Audrey Saunders's Gin-Gin Mule—Tanqueray London dry gin, lime juice, homemade ginger beer, simple syrup, and mint—which is a modern classic.

MURPHY SOUR

You've likely heard of pisco, the unaged grape brandy from Peru. Well, you should also get to know Singani. You might call it pisco's Bolivian cousin, as they are both unaged brandies. And it's due for some continued recognition. See, in 2023, after an eight-year campaign, the US Alcohol and Tobacco Tax and Trade Bureau (TTB) finally granted recognition to Singani as a unique type of brandy and a distinctive product of Bolivia. The campaign was spearheaded by award-winning filmmaker Steven Soderbergh, who's been a huge fan of the spirit since his first encounter back in 2007. And what better way to be introduced to this amazing spirit than to sample this drink, made by my friend H. Joseph Ehrmann, owner of Elixir Saloon in San Francisco and a partner with the Fresh Victor juice company. Here's what H. had to say about the Murphy Sour.

In 1984, I befriended an American kid who had spent the previous years in London. His name was Bob Murphy, and he taught me a lot about London at a time that I knew very little. He introduced me to clementines, and though they were widely available in Europe at the time (grown in Spain), they were hard to find in New Jersey . . . [but] now you can get them easily from about November through March. I whipped up this twist on a Pisco Sour while at home, because when they are in season, there is always a bowl of clementines in my house. Thanks, Murph.

I created this drink in 2013 using pisco, but when asked to compete for the second time in the San Francisco World Spirits Competition Cocktail of the Year contest, I chose to enter this recipe with Singani 63 as the main ingredient (one of three spirit options, Singani is an immature brandy from Bolivia that is similar to pisco). I won the contest (defending my 2018 win) alongside Dale DeGroff, who won the Stillhouse Vodka contest, and Gary Gruver, who won the Mezquila contest.

2 ounces Singani 63

¾ ounce fresh clementine, tangerine, or mandarin juice

½ ounce fresh lime juice

1 ounce clover honey syrup (see page 7)

1 tablespoon chopped fresh cilantro, plus 1 cilantro leaf for garnish

¾ ounce egg white

Combine the Singani, clementine juice, lime juice, honey syrup, chopped cilantro, and egg white in a cocktail shaker without ice. Dry shake (see page 4), then add ice to the shaker and shake well for 15 seconds. Strain into a chilled cocktail glass and garnish with the cilantro leaf to look like clover.

MYRTLE BANK PUNCH

This tiki classic was named after the Patio Bar of Jamaica's Myrtle Bank Hotel, which, according to Jeff "Beachbum" Berry's *Potions of the Caribbean*, "was the social epicenter of Kingston in the 1920s and '30s." Both Donn "Don the Beachcomber" Beach and Victor "Trader Vic" Bergeron featured this drink on their respective menus, so it seems both gentlemen spent some time getting "inspired" at the Patio Bar.

Beach had his version of the drink on his 1941 menu, says Berry, while Vic published his in his 1946 *Book of Food and Drink*, in which he called the Myrtle Bank Punch "the most widely publicized drink of the West Indies." Try 'em both and see which one you prefer.

TRADER VIC'S VERSION

makes 1 cocktail

1 teaspoon sugar

½ ounce fresh lime juice

1½ ounces Lemon Hart 151 Demerara rum

1 teaspoon grenadine

⅓ ounce maraschino liqueur, to float

Combine the sugar and the lime juice in a cocktail shaker and stir to dissolve the sugar. Add ice, then add the rum and grenadine and shake well. Strain into a highball glass filled with crushed ice, then float (see page 5) the maraschino liqueur atop the drink.

DON THE BEACHCOMBER'S VERSION

1½ ounces dark Jamaican rum

¾ ounce gold Jamaican rum

¾ ounce fresh lime juice

¾ ounce fresh white grapefruit juice

¾ ounce Don's honey mix (2:1 honey and water)

¾ ounce soda water

2 dashes Angostura bitters

Combine all the ingredients in a cocktail shaker filled with ice. Shake well and strain into a Collins glass filled with crushed ice.

NAVY GROG

Many drink origin stories begin with "As the story goes . . ." or "According to legend. . ." Why? Because they're apocryphal. (That's a nice word for it; there's another one that begins with b-u-l-l.) Perhaps my favorite example is how my New Orleans French Creole ancestor Antoine Amédée Peychaud served his proprietary bitters along with Cognac, sugar, and water in an hourglass-shaped egg-cup known in French as a *coquetier*, and that's where the word "cocktail" comes from. Sadly, not true. But the British Royal Navy tradition of "grog" has an airtight, verifiable story behind it. In the eighteenth century, sailors on Royal Navy ships were given a daily allowance of one half pint of rum (or gin) each day. That's eight ounces! Enough to make four Daiquiris! If a sailor were to drink all that in one gulp . . . trouble! Of course, that's often what happened. In his excellent book *Rum: A Social and Sociable History of the Real Spirit of 1776*, Ian Williams wrote that "unsurprisingly, ships did not function well in the immediate aftermath of its distribution," and "the pernicious custom of the seamen drinking their allowance of rum in drams, and often at once, is attended with many fatal effects." What was to be done?

Along came British vice admiral Edward Vernon, who decided to take action to stem "the swinish vice of drunkenness." On August 21, 1740, Vernon issued Order to Captains No. 349, which specified that the daily ration of rum would be diluted with a full quart of water, "to be mixed in a scuttled butt kept for that purpose, and to be done upon the deck, and in the presence of the Lieutenant of the Watch who is to take particular care to see that the men are not defrauded in having their full allowance of rum . . . and let those that are good husbandmen receive extra lime juice and sugar that it be made more palatable to them." Further, it was to be split between two servings, one in the late morning and one in the late afternoon. This practice would serve many purposes: It would obviously dilute the potent rum, but also give the sailors hydration, while making the drinking water safer (in those days, it was often contaminated). And by 1747, the addition of lime juice was proven to be a preventative to scurvy.

This potion came to be known as grog and the twice-daily ritual became a highlight of a sailor's day at sea. But what's up with this "scuttled butt" business? That refers to a disused barrel with a removable lid, and Williams notes that it was "the origin of the term *scuttlebutt* to describe the gossip that went on as the crew lined up for their rations." So where did the term *grog* originate? It seems Admiral Vernon was fond of wearing a coat made of a coarse fabric known as grogram, woven from silk and mohair (or wool). As a result, the sailors not only called *him* "Old Grog," but his rationed drink, as well.

The Royal Navy continued the daily ration of a "tot" of rum (or gin) until July 31, 1970, known forever as Black Tot Day. (One final comment on Vernon: In 1741 he successfully led a British assault on Spanish-held Cuba, resulting in the capture of Guantánamo Bay. One of the infantry regiments under Vernon's command was led by a young Virginian, Captain Lawrence Washington, who admired Vernon so much that after the war he renamed his family farm Mount Vernon. Upon Washington's death in 1752, his younger half brother George inherited the estate and retained the name. Small world, right? In the 1790s, George would operate a very prosperous distillery at Mount Vernon, making mostly rye whiskey, not rum.)

Here again I'll offer you two different versions of the same drink, by Victor "Trader Vic" Bergeron and Donn "Don the Beachcomber" Beach, the principal leaders of the tiki bar movement of the 1930s. The Trader Vic's version was a favorite of president Richard Nixon, who used to sneak out of the White House for a quick one; there was a Trader Vic's in the Hilton Hotel just a couple of blocks north. Interestingly enough, Martin Cate (see page 186) got his first glimpse of, and inspiration for, the world of tiki at that very Trader Vic's. Meanwhile, Frank Sinatra favored the Don the Beachcomber Navy Grog, and would have one made by legendary tiki bartender Tony Ramos (see page 90) whenever he visited their outpost in Palm Springs.

recipe continues →

TRADER VIC'S VERSION

makes 1 cocktail

2 ounces dark rum (such as Angostura 7 year)

1 ounce gold rum (Angostura's 1919 Deluxe Blend is perfect in this one)

¾ ounce fresh lime juice

¾ ounce honey syrup (see page 7)

½ ounce fresh grapefruit juice

¼ ounce St. Elizabeth allspice dram

Combine all the ingredients in a cocktail shaker filled with ice and shake well. Strain into an Old-Fashioned glass in which a cone of ice has been placed (grab a Navy Grog Ice Cone Kit from CocktailKingdom.com), with a hole for a straw.

DON THE BEACHCOMBER'S VERSION

makes 1 cocktail

½ ounce fresh lime juice

½ ounce fresh white grapefruit juice

½ ounce club soda

½ ounce gold rum (such as Angostura's 1919 Deluxe Blend)

½ ounce dark rum (such as Angostura 7 year)

½ ounce white rum

½ ounce honey syrup (see page 7)

Combine all the ingredients in a cocktail shaker filled with ice and shake well. Strain into an Old-Fashioned glass packed with shaved or crushed ice (or use an ice cone; see above).

PAINKILLER

For all of its deliciousness, this drink has ironically caused more pain and controversy than you might think. It was invented at the Soggy Dollar Bar in the British Virgin Islands, circa 1980, but accounts are a bit sketchy as to who invented it. Located within the Sandcastle resort on the island of Jost Van Dyke, the bar got its name simply because the resort hadn't gotten around to building a dock at which visiting boats could tie up. So, many boaters would drop anchor and swim ashore to wet their whistles—and wet their money on the swim in. Thus the name "Soggy Dollar." But that's not the painful part; in fact, that sounds pretty pleasant.

The Pusser's Rum Company started bottling their own version of the Painkiller in 1988. Then, Pusser's registered the name and label as a US trademark, and in 2003 they registered the term PAINKILLER, as used in "alcoholic fruit drinks with fruit juices and cream of coconut and coconut juice," as a US trademark. Armed with these and other trademarks, the company then sought to "educate" bartenders and consumers that in order to make a proper Painkiller, you had to use Pusser's. This campaign ended up causing a considerable amount of pain for both Pusser's and the owners of a bar named Painkiller in New York, Richard Boccato and Giuseppe González.

What sometimes muddies the water is the fact that there's some dispute over who invented the drink, and when. But in trademark law, that's not necessarily the controlling factor. See, it doesn't matter who was the first to *use* a name; it's the longest *continuous user* of a mark that holds the trademark rights. If that party is Pusser's, then they're the trademark owner. The Painkiller trademark dispute is painfully (sorry) illustrative as to how one can be "in the right," legally, but still end up in a public relations pickle when they try to enforce those rights. Pain aside, this is a sheer pleasure to drink.

recipe continues →

1½ ounces Pusser's rum

1½ ounces pineapple juice

¾ ounce crème of coconut (I like Coco Reàl cream of coconut)

½ ounce fresh orange juice

Freshly grated nutmeg, for garnish

Combine the rum, pineapple juice, crème of coconut, and orange juice in a cocktail shaker filled with ice and shake well. Strain into a large snifter filled with crushed ice. Grate some nutmeg atop the drink and serve with a straw.

PALOMA

Think of this drink as a simplified Margarita, or a "training wheels" version of that drink. Indeed, its simplicity makes this a very popular drink on either side of the border. The funny thing about the Paloma (the Spanish word for "dove," by the way), is that while some classic drinks started off "pure," and got corrupted, it's the other way around for the Paloma. Take the Daiquiri, for example. It started out with freshly squeezed lime juice, sugar, and rum. Simple, all natural. Then along came artificial flavorings and colorings and sweeteners, and it was a mess (and in some places, still is). But then the craft cocktail renaissance came along and we're getting back to making it the original, natural way.

Au contraire with the Paloma, it seems. Going back to the 1950s, advertisements for Squirt grapefruit soda were telling people to simply mix tequila with their fine product, et voilà—you had yourself a tasty drink (and it actually is, and if that's all you have on hand, go for it!). Only in relatively recent years have craft bartenders been taking the trouble to make the drink with fresh lime juice and house-made grapefruit soda. Be sure to thank your bartenders for their attention to detail next time you have one of these when you're out on the town. Come to think of it, perhaps the Paloma is not unlike the Gimlet (page 99), where the original and authentic version of drink isn't necessarily the *best* version of the drink.

recipe continues →

2 ounces tequila

½ ounce fresh lime juice

Pinch of salt (optional)

2 ounces grapefruit soda, store-bought (such as San Pellegrino or another brand with real fruit flavoring) or homemade (see Note)

1 grapefruit peel, for garnish (optional)

This drink can be shaken or built in the glass.

Here's the first way: Combine the tequila, lime juice, and salt (if using) in a cocktail shaker filled with ice. Shake well and strain into a Collins glass filled with ice. Rinse the shaker (see page 5) with the grapefruit soda, then strain the soda into the drink. Garnish with the grapefruit peel, if desired.

Here's the second: Pour the lime juice into a Collins glass, then fill the glass with ice. Add the tequila, salt (if using), and grapefruit soda, then stir. Garnish with the grapefruit peel, if desired.

---

note: To make your own grapefruit soda, simply mix ½ ounce fresh grapefruit juice, ½ ounce simple syrup (see page 6), and about 3 ounces soda water.

PAPER PLANE

This is one of the great contemporary Sour cocktails, and I asked its creator, Sam Ross, for background. Sam invented the drink circa 2008 when he was working at the legendary Milk & Honey in New York. Sam created it at the request of his friend and former colleague Toby Maloney, who'd worked with Sam at Milk & Honey and had now opened his own bar, the Violet Hour, in Chicago. He then relayed the drink recipe to Maloney "via a 'slightly buzzed three-a.m. voicemail.' When Maloney played the message, he misheard the name as 'The Paper Airplane.'" And that's how the drink originally appeared on the Violet Hour's menu. Ross further explained that the "cocktail is named after the M.I.A. track that was blasting on repeat the summer we worked on the drink."

It's interesting to note that the original recipe called for Campari, but Ross later decided it was too bitter, and he wanted to balance it out with a little sweetness. So, he used Aperol in place of the Campari "and was immediately satisfied with the result." While creating the drink, Sam was inspired by the Last Word (page 124) and its delicate balance of citrus, herbal liqueur, and spirit. Whether you make it with Campari or Aperol, it's a tremendous drink, and will also introduce you to the wonderful qualities of Amaro Nonino, and amari in general.

recipe continues →

¾ ounce bourbon

¾ ounce Amaro Nonino Quintessentia

¾ ounce Aperol

¾ ounce fresh lemon juice

Combine all the ingredients in a cocktail shaker filled with ice. Shake well and strain into a chilled cocktail glass.

variations: Add a little mint, and you've got the Amen Corner, created by Nick Brown. Or use Japanese whisky, Martini Fiero vermouth, Amaro Nonino, fresh lemon juice, and yuzu syrup, and you've made a Paper Crane, invented by Sam Lee in Boston. Or use Mezcal, yellow Chartreuse, Aperol, and lime juice to make Joaquín Simó's Naked and Famous, which Joaquín describes as "the bastard love child of the classic Last Word and Paper Plane, conceived in the mountains of Oaxaca." (God, I love that line . . .)

PARASOL

The classic Daiquiri has served as the springboard of inspiration for so, so many great drinks, among them the Mai Tai (page 138), and most other tiki drinks that rely on the classic platform of rum, lime juice, and sugar. The Parasol is another in this canon. It was invented by Shannon Mustipher, author of *Tiki: Modern Tropical Cocktails* and beverage director at Gladys Caribbean in Crown Heights, Brooklyn (see the Sichuan Sour, page 199). She calls it her "signature Daiquiri," and explains that it came about as one of those moments of serendipity when a random occurrence sparked creativity.

Shannon was enjoying a drink at her favorite local bar, King Tai in Brooklyn. In walked a friend who happened to own a jam company called Brins Jams. The friend gave Shannon a jar of handmade banana jam. In a great article on Flaviar.com, Shannon explained: "Without batting an eyelash," she "handed it over to the bartender and rattled off a drink spec: aged white rum, pineapple juice, the jam, and lime juice." And thus, a modern classic was born.

makes 1 cocktail

2 ounces aged white rum (such as Probitas or Denizen)

¾ ounce fresh lime juice

½ ounce banana liqueur or chef-grade banana puree (such as Boiron or Perfect Puree)

½ ounce pineapple juice

Freshly grated nutmeg, for garnish

Combine the rum, lime juice, banana liqueur, and pineapple juice in a cocktail shaker filled with ice. Shake well and strain into a chilled cocktail glass. Garnish the top of the drink with freshly grated nutmeg.

PEGU CLUB

This was the house drink at the Pegu Club, a British Officers Club in Yangon, Myanmar (formerly Rangoon, Burma) over a century ago. We first see recipes for the drink in 1927's *Barflies and Cocktails* by Harry MacElhone, owner of Harry's New York Bar (Paris), and in Harry Craddock's *The Savoy Cocktail Book* three years later. Craddock noted that the drink is "one that has traveled, and is asked for, round the world." Still is. However, in each of these recipes, the amount of lime juice (1 teaspoon) hardly qualified the drink for "Sour" status.

Contemporary recipes, such as the version made at Audrey Saunders's late lamented Pegu Club in New York's Soho, have increased the citrus component considerably. Saunders uses a specific recipe, as is her wont. She put "dozens and dozens of hours" it, and the resulting drink is pretty amazing.

makes 1 cocktail

2 ounces Tanqueray London dry gin (for its "juniper-forward base")

¾ ounce Marie Brizard orange curaçao ("still the ideal," per Audrey)

¾ ounce fresh lime juice

1 or 2 dashes Angostura bitters

1 dash Pegu Club house bitters (see Note)

1 lime wedge, for garnish

Combine the gin, curaçao, lime juice, Angostura bitters, and Pegu Club bitters in a cocktail shaker filled with ice. Shake well and strain into a chilled cocktail glass. Garnish with the lime wedge.

> **note:** Pegu Club's house bitters are a 1:1 mix of Gary Regan's and Fee Brothers orange bitters, the combination of which Audrey explained "had the angels singing." Sadly, both Gary and Joe Fee passed away within months of each other, in late 2019 and early 2020, respectively, and they're singing with the angels today.

variation: Back in the mid-1990s, while tending bar at the Townhouse Bar & Grill in Emeryville, California, Paul Harrington was challenged by a customer/friend named Matt Jasmin to make something he'd never made before. Paul decided to make a riff on the Pegu, but used lemon, not lime, and substituted a bit of Campari for the two bitters. The result was the Jasmine (a lovely name, no doubt, but apparently Paul misspelled Matt's last name). The amazing thing about this drink is that the combination of Cointreau and Campari results in the pronounced flavor of grapefruit juice (!). Indeed, when I'm making a Hemingway Daiquiri for someone who should avoid grapefruit (because of cholesterol meds), I use this same trick (see page 77). Here's Harrington's Jasmine:

JASMINE

makes 1 cocktail

1½ ounces London dry gin

¾ ounce fresh lemon juice

½ ounce Campari

¼ ounce Cointreau

1 lemon peel, for garnish

Combine the gin, lemon juice, Campari, and Cointreau in a cocktail shaker filled with ice and shake well. Strain into a chilled cocktail glass and garnish with the lemon peel.

PENICILLIN

If there's one drink that embodies the concepts of this book (namely, that a great drink platform can be used to create great *new* drinks, and that it doesn't take a world-class bartender to figure it out), it's the Penicillin. This drink is a riff on a riff on the classic. Don't get me wrong, the inventor is a world-class bartender, and the creator of the original drink on which the first riff was based was *also* a world-class bartender. But the guy who dreamed up the initial riff? He was but a friend and partner of a world-class bartender. Allow me to explain.

The Penicillin was invented by Sam Ross (see page 169) at the original location of Milk & Honey in New York City, circa 2005. Sam had only arrived in the States the year before and found himself working with the great Sasha Petraske, the bar's founder and owner. One day, John Glaser, founder of Compass Box Scotch Whisky, had just dropped off a batch of their fine products for the bartenders to get to know. Sam decided to use some of that whisky to make a variation on the Gold Rush cocktail (see page 43). Remember, the Gold Rush is the drink that a customer, T. J. Siegal, suggested Petraske make, and which was originally based on a couple of classics (depending on your perspective). After all, you could think of the Gold Rush as a Whiskey Sour (page 229), but made with honey syrup, or a Bee's Knees (page 42) with bourbon in place of the gin. So, you have a classic (or two) inspiring a modern classic, which inspired yet another modern classic. *Phew.* Standing on the shoulders of giants, indeed.

According to Robert Simonson's 2016 book *A Proper Drink*, Ross used the Compass Box Asyla bottling as the base of his drink, then decided to sweeten it with a mixture of honey and the bar's house ginger syrup, to provide sweetness with some bite. Although Ross was happy with the finished product, he decided it wasn't done. He then floated a barspoon of Compass Box Peat Monster atop the drink (see page 5), and declared victory. "That smoke stayed on the top. I preferred to never serve it with a straw," Ross said. "I want that smoke in the nose and that spicy-sweet cocktail underneath."

But it's not like the drink then went viral. No, it remained somewhat obscure for a while longer. Fast-forward nine months: Sam was working at nearby Little Branch, another of Petraske's bars in New York City. A waitress, Lucinda Sterling, encouraged Ross to make a Penicillin for a table of hers that had asked for what he called "Bartender's Choices." "She said I should put a Penicillin out because every table needs to experience one of them," Ross recalled. "It wasn't until she said that, that I was like, 'Oh, maybe there's something there.'" In 2007, Ross traveled to Los Angeles to do some consulting work and found himself "planting the seed of the drink in bars there." As more and more bartenders took notice of the Penicillin, its popularity grew, and within a few years, it had become established as a modern classic.

makes 1 cocktail

2 ounces blended Scotch

¾ ounce Honey-Ginger Syrup (recipe follows)

¾ ounce fresh lemon juice

¼ ounce single-malt Scotch (the peatier or smokier, the better)

Candied ginger, for garnish

Combine the blended Scotch, honey-ginger syrup, and lemon juice in a cocktail shaker filled with ice and shake well. Strain into an Old-Fashioned glass with 1 large ice cube. Using a barspoon, float the Scotch atop the drink (see page 5). Garnish with the candied ginger.

recipe continues →

HONEY-GINGER SYRUP

1 cup honey

1 (6-inch) piece fresh ginger, peeled and sliced

In a small saucepan, combine the honey, ginger, and 1 cup water and bring to a boil over high heat. Reduce the heat to maintain a simmer and cook for 5 minutes. Let cool, then cover and refrigerate overnight. Strain the syrup into a clean bottle or airtight container; discard the solids. Cover and store in the refrigerator. It should keep for several weeks.

PERDIDO SOUR

This recipe was offered to me by one of my earliest friends in the cocktail world and one of my greatest mentors, Dale DeGroff. Way back in August 2004, I was fortunate enough to be invited to present at the Tales of the Cocktail festival in New Orleans. Sensing we had some things in common, Ann Tuennerman, the event's founder, introduced me to Dale and his lovely and talented wife, Jill. From there I'd get to know Anistatia Miller, Jared Brown, Ted Haigh, Robert Hess, and Chris and Laura McMillian. By year's end, the eight of us went on to found the Museum of the American Cocktail in New Orleans. It is a fixture in the cocktail scene, and we've remained good friends ever since.

Dale isn't called "King Cocktail" for nothing. I cannot think of anyone, living or dead, over the past forty years who's done more to reestablish the cocktail as a cultural and culinary institution, from the perspective of teaching and mentoring about how drinks are properly made to the history and folklore behind the great drinks. In the past ten or so years, he's launched some amazing new products, from his award-winning Pimento Bitters to his two recent offerings, DeGroff Bitter Aperitivo and DeGroff New World Amaro. They're both sensational, and this simple yet sophisticated drink highlights the Bitter Aperitivo beautifully.

recipe continues →

1½ ounces BarSol Pisco Italia

¾ ounce DeGroff Bitter Aperitivo

¾ ounce Triple Syrup (recipe follows)

½ ounce egg white

⅜ ounce fresh lemon juice

⅜ ounce fresh lime juice

3 dashes Angostura bitters

Combine the pisco, Bitter Aperitivo, triple syrup, egg white, lemon juice, and lime juice in a cocktail shaker filled with ice. Shake well and strain into a chilled cocktail glass. Dash the bitters atop the foam of the drink.

TRIPLE SYRUP

3 ounces agave syrup

2 ounces simple syrup (see page 6)

1 ounce honey syrup (see page 7)

Combine all three syrups in a small bowl or large measuring cup, then transfer to a clean airtight bottle or container. Cover and store in the refrigerator. It should keep for several weeks.

PISCO PUNCH

Sometimes things just line up well. In June 2023, I happened to be in Las Vegas to attend a trademark licensing expo, definitely *not* a cocktail jaunt. But I learned through a friend that bartending legend and longtime friend Tony Abou-Ganim was hosting a tasting of La Madrina's excellent line of Peruvian piscos at Libertine Social Mandalay Bay, where Tony is a partner. I attended the tasting and enjoyed the Pisco Punch that Tony offered to the crowd. It was predictably delicious, and he offered both his recipe and some comments on the drink:

I have long loved Peruvian pisco, and even though the Pisco Punch takes a little extra work to prepare the pineapple gum and press fresh pineapples for juice, I think it is well worth it! Spending much of my formative years in San Francisco, from 1985 to 1998, I have had a love affair with the Pisco Punch for a long time, and it's great to see bartenders gravitating back to this lost classic as well as embracing the beauty that is Peruvian pisco and its culture.

The Pisco Punch is a pre-Prohibition classic that's especially legendary in San Francisco. According to Guillermo L. Toro-Lira and David Wondrich's excellent contribution in *The Oxford Companion to Spirits and Cocktails*, punch made with Pisco was a common beverage in Peru dating back to 1791; note, however, it was nothing more than Pisco, lemon juice, sugar, and water. It was a San Francisco bartender by the name of Duncan "Pisco John" Nicol, who worked at the city's Bank Exchange Saloon from 1893 until Prohibition, who elevated the Pisco Punch served in the City by the Bay to immortality. While we do know that he added pineapple to the flavor profile, there was something different about his Pisco Punch that made it, well, *special*. What was so distinctive about Pisco John's version? It remained a guarded secret. According to the *Oxford Companion* article, "Those who tried the drink found it extraordinarily exhilarating and 'propulsive,'" and a report in 1912 noted that "one authority claims one punch 'will make a gnat fight an elephant.' Others maintain it floats them in the region of bliss of hasheesh [sic] or absinthe." Upon Nicol's death in 1926, an obituary referred to his Punch as "ambrosial drink" that "softened all asperities, soothed every anguish of the hurt mind, stirred the imagination, and seemed to make the whole world kin."

What could have been ol' Pisco John's secret formula? Could it have been *cocaine*? While nothing's been proven, there is a decent case for this conclusion. Indeed, as the article continues, "Tonics and syrups containing cocaine were very popular from the 1860s to the 1890s; Vin Mariani used coca leaves from Peru in its tonic wine, and Coca-Cola also used them in early production. These concoctions were declared illegal in 1914, and their use in the Pisco Punch may have given Nicol reason to keep the recipe secret until his death."

Not to fear, dear reader—the recipe here contains no such contraband ingredients, but I do promise it'll make you a truly delicious drink. Here's the Pisco Punch that Tony Abou-Ganim served us that day.

makes 1 cocktail

2 ounces La Madrina Pisco Torontel

1 ounce pineapple gum syrup, homemade (recipe follows) or store-bought (from Liber & Co.)

1 ounce fresh lemon juice

1 ounce pineapple juice (Tony suggests Dole)

Combine all the ingredients in a cocktail shaker filled with ice. Shake well and strain into a chilled cocktail glass.

PINEAPPLE GUM SYRUP

4 ounces gum arabic powder

3 cups cane sugar

1 medium whole, ripe pineapple, peeled, cored, and chopped into small pieces

In a medium bowl, mix the gum arabic powder and ½ cup water with a fork for about 2 minutes, pressing down with the fork to dissolve any clumps. Cover with plastic wrap and let stand at room temperature overnight.

The next day, combine the sugar, pineapple chunks, and 1½ cups water in a large saucepot. Bring to a simmer over medium heat, breaking up the pineapple chunks with a potato masher and stirring to dissolve the sugar. Remove from the heat and let stand for 4 hours.

Reheat the syrup over medium heat until warm, then strain it through a fine-mesh sieve into the bowl with the gum arabic mixture, pressing on the solids with the back of a spoon to extract as much liquid as possible; discard the solids. Whisk the syrup for 1 minute, let stand for 5 minutes, then whisk again for 1 minute more. Transfer to a clean bottle or airtight container. Cover and store in the refrigerator. It will keep for up to 1 month.

PISCO SOUR

The Pisco Sour was likely invented around 1920 by the owner of the Morris Bar in Lima, Peru, by an American by the name of Victor "Gringo" Morris. He was raised a Mormon in Salt Lake City and traveled to Lima in 1904 to work on the new railroad. He opened the Morris Bar in 1916, where he served his own local variation on the popular Whiskey Sour (page 229). When Morris died in 1929, so did his bar. However, several of his bartenders found work behind the bar at the posh Hotel Maury and brought the drink with them. Yet while the bar became a local institution, the drink was known only regionally for many decades.

Pisco is an unaged grape brandy distilled from wine made from local grape varieties, namely Quebranta, Negra Criolla, Uvina, Mollar, Italia, Torontel, Moscatel, or Albilla. But it's only been in the past twenty years or so that pisco and the Pisco Sour have established themselves on the world stage. The Pisco Sour, the Pisco Punch (page 179), and the spirit itself likely got their first boost in recognition in 1951, when Charles H. Baker Jr. wrote about them in *The South American Gentleman's Companion*: "But in Peru *Pisco*—they call it '*PEES*-ko' there—is a clear white oddly fragrant new grape brandy used both in notable drinks." And due to long-standing trade between Peru and San Francisco, pisco and both drinks have been a fixture in the Bay Area for many years.

Novelist Ernest Hemingway first encountered both pisco and the Pisco Sour in early 1956, when he was in Peru to film some of the fishing scenes for the movie *The Old Man and the Sea*. Although Hemingway loved to travel and fish, he saw the junket as a "waste of time," and an expensive one, to boot. But he did enjoy at least *some* of his time there—predictably, in a bar. While operating out of the Cabo Blanco Fishing Club, Hemingway not only drank pisco, but he "set the record" for the number of Pisco Sours he knocked back. The club's owner, Alfred C. Glassell Jr., noted that "Hemingway did a lot of drinking. . . . That's one of the reasons we were glad to get him down to the club. His bar bill kept us operating for a year. As the owner of the club I *had* to say I was very happy about that."

Lastly, note that Peru celebrates National Pisco Sour Day the first weekend of February each year, but no one says you have to wait until then to enjoy one.

makes 1 cocktail

2 ounces pisco

¾ ounce fresh lime juice (the drink is nice with lemon juice, too)

½ ounce simple syrup (see page 6)

1 medium egg white

2 or 3 dashes Angostura bitters or Peruvian bitters

Combine the pisco, lime juice, simple syrup, and egg white in a cocktail shaker without ice. Dry shake (see page 4), then add ice and shake very well for 15 seconds. Strain the drink into a chilled cocktail glass, then dash the bitters atop the foam to create an interesting pattern.

variation: If you visit Francis Schott's Stage Left Steak in New Brunswick, New Jersey, check out the Parasol cocktail, one of the house specialties (no relation to Shannon Mustipher's Parasol, page 171). It's made with pisco, Aperol, simple syrup, lemon juice, lime juice, and egg white, with Angostura bitters dashed on the foam, just like the Pisco Sour.

PLANTER'S PUNCH

As I learned while researching my book on the Manhattan, some of the most interesting drinks-related stuff is found in nineteenth-century newspapers and magazines. Submitted for your approval, this little poem found in the September 4 edition of the British weekly magazine *Fun*:

> Planters Punch! A West Indian Recipe.
> A wine-glass with lemon juice fill,
> Of sugar the same glass fill twice,
> Then rub them together until,
> The mixture looks smooth, soft, and nice.
> Of rum then add three wine glassfuls,
> And four of cold water please take. A
> Drink then you'll have that's not bad,
> At least, so they say in Jamaica.

Not exactly poetry worthy of Shakespeare, Byron, Shelley, or Keats, but it does describe a pretty tasty libation. Planter's Punch is more or less the unofficial drink of Jamaica. In truth, it's not that there's one specific recipe; rather, Planter's Punch is more of a category. In fact, in his 1939 book *The Gentleman's Companion*, Charles H. Baker Jr. offered *ten* "West Indian Planter's Punches, Swizzles and like ceremonies of a pleasant nature. Any set rules for these tropical institutions would last about as long as a set rule for a mint julep to please (both) Louisville and Baltimore. There are as many Planter's Punches as there are—or were—planters; as many Swizzles as swizzlers." Well said, Mr. Baker.

The recipe I offer here, which Baker claimed was "the original receipt [*sic*] from the very first discovery of the drink," is one he called "The Standard One, Two, Three, Four West Indian Planter's Punch No. 1," as in one part sour, two parts sweet, three parts strong, and four parts weak.

1 ounce fresh lime juice

2 ounces simple syrup (see page 6)

3 ounces dark Jamaican rum

Angostura bitters

Combine the lime juice, simple syrup, rum, and 4 ounces water in a cocktail shaker filled with ice. Then, as Baker instructs, "doctor this with the usual dash of Angostura." Shake well and strain into a tall glass filled with ice.

PORT OF GÖTEBORG

Martin Cate is one of the leading lights in today's tiki cocktail scene. He's the author (with his wife, Rebecca) of *Smuggler's Cove: Exotic Cocktails, Rum, and the Cult of Tiki* (2016), and is co-owner and/or partner in several great tiki venues, namely, Smuggler's Cove in San Francisco; Max's South Seas Hideaway in Grand Rapids, Michigan; California Gold in San Rafael, California; Hala Pele in Portland, Oregon; and False Idol in San Diego. Somewhere along the way he was asked to create a drink for a band in Sweden, and he named it after the port city of Gothenburg, Sweden's second-largest city. With respect to his creative process, Martin tells me:

> The Swedish band Ìxtahuele, an absolutely terrific exotica combo from Gothenburg, commissioned me to come up with a cocktail for their 2016 album *Call of the Islands*. Hailing from a port city, they have always been drawn to tales of the sea and distant ports of call. I went with the Swedish spelling of their town for the name of the drink. I'd years ago made a riff on the Polynesian Paralysis cocktail called the Norwegian Paralysis that swapped out the rum for aquavit, and I loved how well it played with typical tropical cocktail ingredients. So, I dove in again but added Swedish Punsch, an ingredient that also owes its legacy to trade routes through the East Indies. The recipe was also designed to go in a signature tiki mug that they released at the same time by artist Tiki Diablo. It's a great mug that uniquely had a ridge running down the back and came with a big swizzle stick so you could play the mug as a percussion instrument like a güiro. Pretty cool! The recipe has only been printed in the liner notes to the CD as far as I know.

2 ounces aged medium-bodied blended dark rum
(Martin prefers Appleton Estate Reserve 8 year)

1 ounce Swedish punsch (Martin prefers Kronan)

1 ounce fresh lemon juice

¾ ounce passion fruit syrup

¼ ounce aquavit

¼ ounce honey syrup (see page 7)

1 dash Angostura bitters

2 ounces soda water

Several mint sprigs, for garnish

Combine the rum, punsch, lemon juice, passion fruit syrup, aquavit, honey syrup, bitters, and 12 ounces crushed ice in a blender and blend for 3 seconds. Add the soda water, then transfer the contents of the blender to a 22-ounce snifter (or another suitably large glass). Add fresh crushed ice to fill the glass, then garnish with the mint sprigs.

QUEEN'S PARK SWIZZLE

This drink was a longtime staple at Trader Vic's. (On the Trader Vic's drink menu, he described it as the "Toast of the Caribbean, Dark, rich Rums and Tropical Fruits make this a potent but palatable drink.") In fact, the recipe shown below first appeared in Victor Bergeron's 1946 book *Trader Vic's Book of Food and Drink*, in which he urged folks to visit "the Queen's Park Hotel, in Trinidad, whose Queen's Park Swizzle is the most delightful form of anesthesia given out today." He also referred to it as "a world-famous drink . . . that has helped to popularize rum."

The hotel opened in the tony Queen's Park Savannah neighborhood of Port of Spain, Trinidad, in 1895. While the hotel had a decent trade during its first two decades, it really enjoyed a booming business during Prohibition as Americans flocked to destinations in the Caribbean (notably Havana), London, Paris, and elsewhere, seeking to find a good drink. And this is one of them. In the 1972 revised version of his *Trader Vic's Bartender's Guide*, Bergeron noted that "if you like to make and drink a real doozer of a rum drink that really is a rum drink, try this." A final note: In his excellent contribution on the drink in *The Oxford Companion to Spirits and Cocktails*, Jeff "Beachbum" Berry refers to it as "a high-octane cousin of the Mojito." And who am I to argue with either of these two gentlemen?

½ large lime

6 to 8 mint leaves, plus 1 mint sprig for garnish

3 ounces Demerara rum

½ ounce simple syrup (see page 6)

Squeeze ½ ounce of juice from the lime half into a pint glass, then cut the squeezed half into 2 wedges and drop them into the glass. Add the mint leaves. Fill the glass with shaved or crushed ice. Add the rum and simple syrup and swizzle (see page 4) the drink until the glass frosts. Garnish with the mint sprig.

variations: There are so, so many great swizzles out there to try, including the Jamaica Rum Swizzle (Jamaican dark rum, lime juice, simple syrup, mint), the Barbados Red Rum Swizzle (Barbados rum, lime juice, Angostura bitters, sugar), and the Martinique Swizzle (Martinique rum, lemon juice, Angostura, sugar, Pernod).

QUININE SOUR

This is one of the house drinks at Gymkhana, a Michelin-starred Indian restaurant in the Mayfair section of London. The drink is an homage to the gin & tonic, which originated in India when it was a British colony; it was referred to as "the drink most patronized in India" way back in 1881. So think of this as the G&T mashed up with a classic Sour cocktail.

As discussed on page 193, the gin & tonic was an essential part of life in British colonial India, for both therapeutic and social reasons. The G&T came to be one of the most popular drinks of the twentieth century, and remains so today; in fact, it's become something of the national drink in Spain, where it's treated as a blank canvas for innovation, with all kinds of delicious syrups, liqueurs, amaro, aperitivo, and other flavorings being added to the drink. Its popularity in the years after Prohibition was no doubt enhanced by inclusion in Charles H. Baker Jr.'s 1939 book *The Gentleman's Companion*. He described the drink as having been "originated to combat fevers, real or alleged, & which later became an established drink in India & the tropical British East, and still later became acceptable over here by American hosts who wanted to impress folk with having combed the Orient." Baker, ever snarky, then proceeded to chide the British a wee bit for their drinking habits, by noting, "All Americans, and some Britishers not so hidebound as to insist on brassy, half-warm drinks, added 2 lumps of ice, and a twist of lime peel."

In this drink, the curry leaves and ginger offer a delicious complement to the acidity of the lemon juice, and the creamy texture of the egg white. This drink is well worth the (slight) trouble of purchasing curry leaves and tonic bitters, as once you taste this delicious cocktail, you'll want to use them again.

3 thin slices ginger, peeled and chopped

4 fresh curry leaves

2 ounces London dry gin

1 ounce fresh lemon juice

½ ounce simple syrup (see page 6)

3 dashes tonic bitters (such as The Bitter Truth)

1 medium egg white, or ⅓ ounce aquafaba (see page 10)

Combine the ginger, 3 of the curry leaves, gin, lemon juice, simple syrup, and bitters and muddle well. Add the egg white and dry shake (see page 4), then add ice to the shaker and shake well for 20 seconds. Strain the drink into a chilled cocktail glass and garnish with the remaining curry leaf.

DRINK TO YOUR HEALTH: THE THERAPEUTIC ROLE OF QUININE

Wherever you have a hot and humid climate, with monsoon seasons and low-lying areas with standing water, you're going to have mosquitos—and with mosquitos comes malaria. Dating back to the 1600s, Jesuit missionaries in South America noticed that the indigenous peoples of Peru, Bolivia, and Ecuador—the Quechua, the Cañari, and the Chimú, respectively—chewed on the bark of a certain tree to treat fever and chills. According to folklore (and where would a cocktail book be without folklore?), in 1631, the countess of Chinchon, a noblewoman married to a Spanish colonial official, came down with a severe case of malaria. She was given a concoction made by these Jesuit priests from the ground powder from the bark of this particular type of tree. She miraculously recovered, and the tree was named in her honor, the *cinchona* tree. While the story itself is dubious (there was indeed a countess by that name, but her diaries don't speak of her ever having malaria), there is plenty of truth to this treatment becoming the standard therapy.

The active ingredient in the bark came to be known as quinine. Over the centuries that followed, medical researchers devoted a great deal of time and effort in isolating the most favorable varieties of cinchona tree (turns out that *Cinchona pubescens* and *Cinchona calisaya* yield the greatest amounts of quinine). Seeds and cuttings were exported out of South America so other European powers could do further research, as well as cultivate the tree in other regions. By the nineteenth century and into the twentieth, quinine had become the gold standard in the treatment and prevention of malaria. As recently as World War II, the Allies suffered greatly from malaria in the South Pacific, and the Japanese capture of cinchona plantations in Java had a profound effect, as it denied US service personnel the health benefits from the trees' bark.

Initially, quinine was used as a treatment for the symptoms of malaria, namely fever and chills. Then it was discovered that the quinine could be administered prophylactically, almost like a vaccine, to help those who took it from getting a bad case of the dreaded disease.

Okay, so what does any of this have to do with, you know, *drinks*? See, in British colonial India, the daily dose of quinine became part of any British subject's daily regimen, whether in the military or foreign service, or as a merchant. Unfortunately, however, quinine is quite bitter (not so much fun to ingest). But you know the old saying, "just a spoonful of sugar helps the medicine go down"? Those resourceful Brits dreamed up two ways to improve the "delivery system" of their daily dose of quinine.

In 1858, a patent was awarded to Erasmus Bond (that's Bond, Erasmus Bond) for his invention titled "aerated tonic liquid," that is, soda water infused with quinine powder, better known as tonic water. By the 1870s, Schweppes, a chief competitor in the carbonated water category, offered Schweppes Indian Tonic Water. It became a popular product in Britain's tropical colonies, and eventually moved into the American market in 1884.

So, with quinine representing the best defense against malaria, and tonic water offering a palatable delivery system, what was a resourceful (and thirsty) British subject to do to make their daily ration of quinine more tolerable? Add it to gin, of course! And while we're at it, let's add a wedge of lemon or lime, you know, to boost our vitamin C intake—we don't want to get scurvy, now, do we?

A classic quote attributed to Winston Churchill, one of the greatest of all British drinkers, is "The gin and tonic has saved more Englishmen's lives, and minds, than all the doctors in the Empire." I'll drink to that!

RUM-COCO

Back in 2019 I had the honor and pleasure of presenting a cocktail seminar for the Key West Art & Historical Society, on the life and times (and favorite drinks) of celebrated playwright Thomas Lanier "Tennessee" Williams, who lived in Key West for many years (he bought a little cottage there in 1950). While researching his works and biographies to prepare for my seminar, I discovered this lovely little drink. (If you have a moment, you might look up—and even sing!—Tennessee's "drinking anthem," where he sings the praises of having a "little drinkie pie.")

Tennessee first enjoyed this tropical libation while in Acapulco, Mexico, in 1940. He was somewhat marooned at the Hotel Costa Verde, awaiting the arrival of a royalty check. The hotel was teeming with all kinds of interesting characters, from Nazis to war refugees. All things being equal, though, it wasn't such a bad place to be stuck. With time on his hands, Tennessee was inspired by the surroundings to write what ended up being *The Night of the Iguana*, which featured a liberal daily dose of a drink called the Rum-Coco. It was one of the "house drinks" at the hotel's bar. In the play, the protagonist, Shannon, is being pressured by the hotel manager that he had to pay up or get out. What is one to do when facing such a crisis? Get looped, of course! Indeed, that evening Shannon and his friend "had more than our usual quota of rum-cocos, a drink that is prepared in a coconut shell by chopping off one end of it with a machete and mixing the juice of the nut with variable amounts of rum, a bit of lemon juice, a bit of sugar, and some cracked ice," sipped with a straw. Williams observed, "It's a long dreamy drink, the most delectable summer night's drink I've ever enjoyed." The protagonist and his friend would spend the evening in their hammocks sipping rum-cocos "until the stars of the Southern Cross . . . began to flit crazily about like fireflies caught in a bottle."

Within the story, the drink is made with an actual coconut, the top lopped off by a machete. In one scene, Shannon runs through the checklist of items he'll need to make one: "Coconut? Check. Machete? Check. Rum? Double check!" Fear not, I'm not expecting you to go hacking up a coconut, but if you *do* possess such skills, as well as a machete and a coconut, go for it. Here's how we made it that night at the Key West Theater; the audience of over one hundred people lapped it up! And, be assured, no attendees were harmed by any machetes. Not on my watch.

makes 1 cocktail

2 ounces light rum (we used Papa's Pilar Blonde)

¾ ounce coconut water

¾ ounce fresh lemon juice

½ ounce Demarara simple syrup (see page 7)

Combine all the ingredients in a cocktail shaker filled with ice. Shake well and strain into a large glass filled with crushed ice. Enjoy with a straw.

SCOFF-LAW

While America was suffering through Prohibition between 1920 and 1933, Harry MacElhone and the boys at Harry's New York Bar in Paris were having a gay old time, not only serving drinks to all of the expat Yanks who'd flocked to the City of Light to bend the ol' elbow, but also dreaming up drinks to poke fun at anything related to Prohibition. For example, to "celebrate" the fact that ships laden with booze from overseas were dropping anchor right at the three-mile territorial limit of US waters, Harry's invented a drink called the Three-Mile Limit. When that boundary was extended to twelve miles, they introduced the Twelve-Mile.

They also created a drink to poke fun at Sergei Voronoff, a Russian doctor who believed that if you implanted the testicles of monkeys into human subjects, it would bring about fountain-of-youth-like results (for the humans, that is, not the poor monkeys!). By 1927, he claimed that he'd successfully performed over one thousand procedures, which would yield "a life span of 125 years and an old age of a few months." It didn't take ol' Harry and the boys long to lampoon Dr. Voronoff. In the 1923 edition of his book *ABC of Mixing Cocktails*, MacElhone introduced the Monkey Gland, containing gin, orange juice, grenadine, and absinthe, noting that it was "invented by the author, and deriving its name from Voronoff's experiments in rejuvenation."

The Scoff-Law is another example of Harry's hijinks. The story begins with a rather serious fellow named Delcevere King, of Quincy, Massachusetts. He didn't drink, and was therefore all-in on Prohibition. He decided that what the world needed right now was a new word to describe "a drinker of liquor made or obtained illegally—a lawless drinker." King claimed to have been inspired by the words of then President Harding, that "lawless drinking is a menace to the republic itself." King staged a contest and offered the less-than-kingly sum of $200 to the winner. The criteria? The "epithet should be preferably one or two syllables" and "it should preferably begin with 's,' since 'S' words have a sting." There were over 25,000 entries "from forty-eight states and several foreign countries."

Two people came up with the word "scofflaw," as in "someone who scoffs at the law." Both were Massachusetts residents, and it's assumed that they split the pot. Just ten days later, the *Chicago Tribune* reported that "Jock, the genial bartender of Harry's New York Bar . . . invented the Scoff-law Cocktail." The report also noted that the cocktail "has already become exceedingly popular among American prohibition dodgers."

Oh, and that quote from President Harding, the bit about "lawless drinking" being "a menace to the republic?" Well, it turns out that Harding was fond of tipping 'em back on occasion, notably when he was out on the links. Indeed, at the Chevy Chase Club just outside of Washington, DC, Harding caused a bit of a kerfuffle when he would do shots of whiskey every few holes while playing golf at the Club. I'm shocked, *shocked!* As an aside, one of our daughters worked at Chevy Chase Club when she was in high school. You'd think they have a plaque about it but she said she never saw one. Oh well . . . The recipe shown here is from the Harry's New York Bar book *Barflies and Cocktails* (1927), by Harry MacElhone.

makes 1 cocktail

1 ounce rye whiskey

1 ounce dry vermouth

½ ounce fresh lemon juice

½ ounce grenadine

1 dash orange bitters

1 cocktail cherry and/or lemon peel, for garnish

Combine the rye, vermouth, lemon juice, grenadine, and bitters in a cocktail shaker filled with ice. Shake well and strain into a chilled cocktail glass. Garnish with the cherry or lemon peel (or both!).

SELECT APERITIVO SOUR

This simple little gem comes from Manuel Schlüssler, a bartender in Lucerne, Switzerland. What I love about this drink is that it's relatively low in alcohol (the trade term is "low-ABV," as in alcohol by volume), and is fairly easy to make, as in, all of the ingredients are "off the shelf." Schlüssler tells me "I love to go crazy and create amazing, complicated drinks. But the crowd pleasers have to be 'simple and sexy.'" While he usually makes most of his syrups in-house, he finds that passion fruit syrup is just too expensive to make so he goes with Monin, which I've always found to be a solid choice as well. He also noted that he "created that drink in summer 2021 when people started asking for low-ABV drinks. Its freshness comes through the acidity and sweetness from the passion fruit and the bitterness of Select Aperitivo. I decided on Select because of its distinctive wine flavor and its wonderful, deep Bordeaux-red color. Campari wouldn't work because it's too sweet." Manuel prefers the "wine touch" of the Select.

makes 1 cocktail

2 ounces Select Aperitivo

1 ounce fresh lime juice

½ ounce Monin passion fruit syrup

1 medium egg white

Combine all the ingredients in a cocktail shaker filled with ice. Shake well and strain into a chilled cocktail glass.

SICHUAN SOUR

This drink is a great introduction to one of the most popular spirits in the world that you likely have never heard of: that would be baijiu (pronounced *bye-j'yo*), which roughly translates to "white liquor" in Mandarin Chinese. Most baijiu is distilled from sorghum, but it can also be made from other grains, typically rice. The techniques deployed in baijiu production vary greatly by region and style, and different styles of baijiu can be as distinct as whiskey is to tequila. What makes baijiu so distinctive is something called qu (pronounced *chew*), a naturally harvested culture of airborne yeasts and other microorganisms. It makes the taste and scent of every baijiu highly specific to the place it was created. Qu also allows Chinese distillers to ferment and distill grains in a solid state, which creates incredible complexity of flavor. I spent a lovely happy hour with Ming River cofounder and baijiu expert Derek Sandhaus, who gave me a thorough overview on this amazing spirit and tasted me through the range of expressions. Thank you, Derek!

The Sichaun Sour was created by Shannon Mustipher as something of a riff on the Parasol (page 171), which she calls her "signature Daiquiri."

makes 1 cocktail

1½ ounces Ming River (strong-aroma) baijiu

½ ounce Rum Fire overproof rum

½ ounce Giffard crème de fruits de la passion (passion fruit liqueur)

1 ounce fresh lime juice

1 ounce pineapple juice

Candied orange peel, or 1 citrus twist, for garnish

Combine the baijiu, rum, passion fruit liqueur, lime juice, and pineapple juice in a cocktail shaker filled with ice. Shake well and strain into a chilled cocktail glass. Garnish with the candied orange peel.

SIDECAR

The Sidecar is one of the all-time classics. David Embury, in *The Fine Art of Mixing Drinks*, places it on the pantheon of cocktails, along with the Martini, Manhattan, Old-Fashioned, Daiquiri, and Jack Rose (note that half of these six are Sours!), yet just a few pages later grouses that it's "the most perfect example I know of a magnificent drink gone wrong." What Mr. Embury was saying was that this drink, in a misguided attempt at simplification, had been reduced over the years to three ingredients (which is correct), used in equal parts (which is not). "This may not be a bad formula for a midafternoon drink, but for an apéritif it is simply horrible because of its sickish sweetness." I have to agree with him. In all Sours, and this one in particular, you need to have balance. That said, the so-called French School calls for equal parts, while the Anglo-American School's ratio is shown in the recipe here.

As is the case with so many classics, there's no one definitive inventor. Stories range from Pat MacGarry at London's Buck's Club to an unnamed bartender at the Carleton Hotel in Cannes, in the South of France, while Embury vaguely states that "it was invented by a friend of mine at a bar in Paris during World War I after the motorcycle sidecar in which the good captain customarily was driven to and from the little bistro where the drink was born and christened." In Lucius Beebe's *The Stork Club Bar Book* (1946), he writes that "so far as fallible human memory can determine," Frank Meier of the Paris Ritz invented it, using "Ritz's own bottling of a vintage 1865 Cognac," which "set one back . . . the equivalent of five American dollars."

It seems we cannot even agree on how the drink came to be named. A syndicated news story from May 1923 observed that "another new cocktail second only in popularity to the monkey gland has been named a 'sidecar' because it takes the imbiber for a ride." Cute. Here's the traditional recipe.

Sugar, for rimming the glass

Lemon wedge, for rimming the glass

1½ ounces Cognac

¾ ounce Cointreau

¾ ounce fresh lemon juice

Pour about 1 teaspoon of sugar onto a small plate. Moisten the rim of a cocktail glass with the lemon wedge, then dip the rim in the sugar to coat. Fill the glass with ice and set aside to chill. Combine the Cognac, Cointreau, and lemon juice in a cocktail shaker filled with ice and shake well. Strain into the prepared glass.

variations: If you're fancying a Scotch version of the Sidecar, it's called the Silent Third, which was popular back in the 1930s when automobiles featured a "silent" third gear in their transmissions. It's found in the 1937 *Café Royal Cocktail Book.* The drink, that is, not the gear. Another variation is the Spitfire, invented by London bartending great Tony Conigliaro, which has Cognac, lemon juice, simple syrup, egg white, peach liqueur, and dry white wine. Or add a touch of light rum to your Sidecar, and you've got the scandalously named Between the Sheets (Cognac, light rum, lemon juice, triple sec), which was all the rage back in the Jazz Age 1920s. Another drink to try is the Loudspeaker, found in *The Savoy Cocktail Book* (1930); it's basically a Sidecar, but London dry gin shares the main stage with the Cognac. Lastly, I recommend the Champs-Élysées, a Sidecar with an added ½ ounce green Chartreuse, and simple syrup in lieu of the orange liqueur, invented by Toby Maloney at Milk & Honey in the 2000s.

SLOE GIN RICKEY

One could argue that a rickey should not be in this book. But I've decided to bend the rules a wee bit, because this particular version of the Rickey is in fact a sour, and it's so damned good. First off, by definition, a classic rickey is not a Sour simply because its creator, a Washington, DC, lobbyist named "Colonel" Joseph Rickey, specifically eschewed the use of sugar in his namesake drink. As he informed the *Brooklyn Daily Eagle* in August 1892, "Any drink with sugar in it heats the blood, while the 'Rickey,' with its blood cooling lime juice, is highly beneficial" on those hot summer days that are common in my home-town. While bending the ol' elbow at Shoomaker's, where the power brokers of the nation's capital met in the waning years of the nineteenth century, Rickey specified that his drink be made with Belle of Nelson bourbon, lime juice, and Apollinaris mineral water. Soon, however, people started making their Rickeys with gin, and that version really took off. The Gin Rickey was one of F. Scott and Zelda Fitzgerald's favorites, and was featured in his 1925 classic *The Great Gatsby*. It's also my dear wife's go-to summertime drink.

But I contend that you *can* consider the subcategory of "Liqueur Rickeys" to be Sours, due to the sweetness brought by the liqueur. This postulate is sup-ported by David Embury in his 1948 primer *The Fine Art of Mixing Drinks*: "In the case of Liqueur Rickeys no sugar is needed, for the liqueur itself is plenty sweet."

Sloe gin is a gin liqueur that is flavored with blackthorn (aka sloe) berries, along with a little sugar. It's enjoying a bit of a renaissance in recent years, with some excellent offerings coming from Fords, Plymouth, Sipsmith, Hayman's, and Gordon's. The Sloe Gin Rickey dates back nearly as far as the original Rickey. A *Chicago Chronicle* article in August 1897 informed readers that "since the introduction of another seductive tipple, sloe gin, made from the sloe and having a low percentage of alcohol, the gin rickey has made rapid strides in public favor when made of this sloe gin, which has a peculiar sweet taste and a deep carmine shade." It remained popular at least through the 1940s, with Embury noting that "the two most common and best-known Rickeys are the Gin Rickey and the Sloe Gin Rickey."

2 ounces sloe gin

1 ounce fresh lime juice

3 to 4 ounces soda (or mineral) water

1 juiced lime hull, for garnish

Combine the gin and lime juice in a cocktail shaker filled with ice and shake well. Strain into a Collins or highball glass. Rinse the shaker (see page 5) with the soda water, then strain the soda into the glass. Garnish with the lime hull.

> **variations:** Try another liqueur—such as apricot, peach, blackberry, cherry, ginger, elderflower, or many others—as your base.

SOUTHSIDE

Similar to the Bee's Knees (page 42), serve this to a friend who says they cannot stand gin. This is one of the most delicious, refreshing cocktails out there. Think of it as a Gin Mojito, or a minty Tom Collins.

It's said to have been the favorite cocktail of Chicago's Southside Gang, run by Al Capone, though this is probably not the case. Like the Jack Rose tale about "Bald Jack" the mobster, it seems that folks like to connect the Mafia to mixology. According to my friend Eric Felten's entry in *The Oxford Companion to Spirits and Cocktails*, the drink likely originated at Snedecor's Tavern on Long Island. They served a sort of gin Mint Julep there, and when that tavern evolved into the Southside Sportsman's Club, folks came to refer to it as "that Southside drink." At some point the drink hopped across the East River to become one of the house specialties at the 21 Club in Midtown Manhattan.

The earliest known recipe for the drink (well, sort of) is found in Hugo Ensslin's 1917 book *Recipes for Mixed Drinks*. See, Ensslin is referring to the carbonated version of the drink, the Southside Fizz, saying that it's "made same as Gin Fizz, adding fresh mint leaves." And how did Ensslin make his Gin Fizz? See here, which I adapted and modified to add the mint.

makes 1 cocktail

2 ounces London dry gin

1 tablespoon confectioners' sugar, or ½ ounce simple syrup (see page 6)

½ ounce fresh lemon juice

½ ounce fresh lime juice

6 mint leaves, plus 1 mint sprig for garnish

Combine the gin, confectioners' sugar, lemon juice, lime juice, and mint leaves in a cocktail shaker filled with ice. Shake well, then strain into a chilled cocktail glass. Garnish with the mint sprig.

variations: To make a Southside Fizz, strain the drink into a Collins or highball glass filled with fresh ice. Rinse the shaker (see page 5) with 3 to 4 ounces soda water, then strain it into the glass and garnish with the mint sprig. If you start off with the Southside but add ½ ounce fresh grapefruit juice, you've got another delicious drink: the Bailey, invented by American socialite and artist Gerald Murphy in the 1920s at Villa America, their home in Cap d'Antibes in the French Riviera. He and his wife, Sara, were best friends with the likes of F. Scott and Zelda Fitzgerald, Pablo Picasso, Ernest Hemingway, John Dos Passos, Dorothy Parker, and a host of other luminaries of the day.

STRAITS SLING

We've all heard of that legendary drink, the Singapore Sling, right? Sure, you saw Johnny Depp and Benicio del Toro slingin' 'em back in the 1998 film *Fear and Loathing in Las Vegas*, right? So, what's the Straits Sling? It's the progenitor of its far more famous descendant, and really the only one between the two of them that's worth a damn, in my view. Why's that? See, at some point over the past fifty or so years, the Singapore Sling became way, way too sweet. To the original Straits Sling core of gin, Bénédictine, fresh lemon juice, Cherry Heering, and Angostura and orange bitters (which resulted in a delicious and balanced cocktail), some genius decided to add orange juice (sweet), pineapple juice (sweet), Cointreau (more sweet), and grenadine (even more sweet). It's a mess, folks—a diabetic coma waiting to happen. The result, in the words of David Wondrich in *The Oxford Companion to Spirits and Cocktails*, "was overtly 'tropical' and perfectly adapted to the disco drink era."

The Singapore Sling is alleged to have been invented in 1915 by a bartender at the Raffles Hotel in Singapore. That said, there is evidence of there being a Singapore Gin Sling or a Straits Sling in existence prior to that. The likely outcome is that the hotel simply "embraced" or "claimed" the drink as their own, and then made up the story about it originating there. Oh, and they also replaced some of the pricier ingredients with cheaper (and sweeter) ones, claiming also that they'd somehow "discovered" the original recipe, and this was it. In a way, it's not unlike the Hurricane (page 107), a drink that, when made correctly, is delicious, but it's no longer made that way where it's said to have been invented. But when made as it was originally made, it's what Charles H. Baker Jr. called "a delicious, slow-acting, insidious thing," a drink that he claims he "met in 1926, & thereafter never forgotten." Got all that?

The recipe shown here is based on the one found in Harry Craddock's *The Savoy Cocktail Book* from 1930.

2 ounces London dry gin

½ ounce dry cherry brandy (either kirsch or Cherry Heering)

½ ounce Bénédictine

½ ounce fresh lemon juice

3 to 4 ounces soda water

1 lemon peel, for garnish

Combine the gin, cherry brandy, Bénédictine, and lemon juice in a cocktail shaker filled with ice. Shake well and strain into a Collins glass filled with ice. Add the soda water to the shaker, swirl it around to chill it (and capture any remaining flavor clinging to the ice), then strain it into the drink and stir. Garnish with the lemon peel.

variations: If you use vodka in place of the gin, and Domaine de Canton ginger liqueur in place of the Bénédictine, you'll have the Cook Strait Sling, a drink invented by yours truly, and co-winner of the 42 Below Cocktail World Cup (Washington, DC, bracket) in 2010. I named the drink for Cook Strait, the passage between the North and South Islands of New Zealand, since the competition was sponsored by 42 Below vodka (a fine New Zealand product). If you keep the London dry gin of the original, it's now a Sin No More Sling, which I also created, while working for Domaine de Canton, and which was featured in Gary Regan's 2009 book *The Bartender's Gin Companion*.

STRAWBERRY DAZE

I encountered this delicious little drink one evening in 2023 while out to dinner with a couple of work colleagues in Las Vegas. We wanted to get "off the Strip," away from the tourists, and I suggested my favorite Italian restaurant in Vegas, Nora's. While waiting for our table, I came to realize that the bartender, Gaston Martinez, and I were old acquaintances. We'd met a few times before at Tales of the Cocktail in New Orleans. Small world!

After we'd been seated, Gaston brought us three of the tastiest Sour cocktails we'd ever had. The unanimous choice as the best of the lot was this one, the Strawberry Daze. While savoring the drink, I noted its frothy texture, and I asked him, "I guess you do a dry shake first to get the egg white emulsified?" He shook his head, "Dry shake, yes, but no egg white. We use aquafaba." I was like, aqua-*what*? I'd been unaware of this cool trick (see page 10) until that time, and my mind was pretty much blown. Of course, it's been a "thing" in the bartending world for years, but it somehow evaded me until that evening. Maybe it's because, you know, *I'm not a real bartender*. Cheers to you, Gaston!

makes 1 cocktail

1 strawberry

3 basil leaves

1½ ounces Absolut Elyx vodka

¾ ounce St-Germain elderflower liqueur

1 ounce fresh lemon juice

¾ ounce simple syrup (see page 6)

¾ ounce aquafaba (see page 10; it also works great with 1 ounce egg white)

Muddle the strawberry and 2 of the basil leaves well in a shaker. Add the vodka, St-Germain, lemon juice, simple syrup, and aquafaba. Dry shake (see page 4), then add ice and shake for 15 seconds. Strain into a chilled cocktail glass and garnish with the remaining basil leaf.

SUFFERING BASTARD

I was introduced to this classic back in 2010, when Derek Brown and I produced a Museum of the American Cocktail seminar in Washington, DC, presented by world-renowned mixologist and cocktail historian Jeff "Beachbum" Berry, titled "The Suffering Bastard: Joe Scialom, International Barman of Mystery." According to Berry's contribution in *The Oxford Companion to Spirits and Cocktails* (2022), Joseph Scialom, born Giuseppe Chalom di fu Isacco, "became the most famous bartender of World War II when his drink the Suffering Bastard purportedly helped with the Second Battle of El Alamein." Of all the drink origin stories in all of the bars in all the world, this one's gotta be near the top.

It seems Scialom, born in Egypt, trained as a chemist; fluent in eight languages, he was tending bar at the world-famous Shepheard's Hotel in Cairo. The hotel's "Long Bar" became something of an officer's club for the British Eighth Army, as well as the Anglo-American press corps covering the campaign against German Field Marshal Erwin Rommel and his vaunted Afrika Korps. In October 1942, after a long evening at the Long Bar, the boys of the Eighth had their hands full against the Nazis and cabled the hotel for a batch of Scialom's "hangover cure" to be sent to the front, *tout de suite!* Scialom obliged, sending four gallons of the drink in Thermos jugs via taxicab to the battle front. According to legend, this "spirited" boost in morale helped turn the tide, and the British were victorious. And, of course, the press ate, er . . . *drank* it up.

Scialom became something of a celebrity, and he parlayed his fame into a long-lasting bartending gig with the Hilton family of hotels, working in San Juan, Puerto Rico, Havana, London, Rome, and New York. But it was the Suffering Bastard that put him on the map. Here's how.

recipe continues →

1 ounce London dry gin

1 ounce brandy

½ ounce lime cordial (see page 9)

2 dashes Angostura bitters

2 to 3 ounces ginger beer

1 orange slice, for garnish

1 mint sprig, for garnish

Combine the gin, brandy, lime cordial, and bitters in a cocktail shaker filled with ice. Shake well and strain into a Collins glass filled with ice. Rinse the shaker (see page 5) with the ginger beer, then strain the ginger beer into the glass. Garnish with the orange slice and mint sprig.

TEMPTATION ISLAND

This next drink supports the idea that you can find a delicious cocktail in places where you might not expect them, and much of this points to the simplicity of the Sour platform. But having a great bartender never hurts, either! During the summer of 2023, my wife, daughters, son-in-law, and I were on holiday in Northern California's Russian River Valley. One day, after a morning of wine tasting, we set off for lunch in Healdsburg. I was still in the thick of writing this book, and was ever vigilant for new discoveries. Can you find a great cocktail in the heart of California wine country? Yes, you can.

We went to a vibrant restaurant in the center of town called Lo & Behold. Sure, they were going to have a tremendous wine selection. But cocktails? I took one look at the drinks menu, then had a glance around at the bar, and I knew immediately—*this place is legit.*

I got to talking with one of the owners, Laura Sanfilippo, and told her about the Sours book I was writing. I asked if they had one (or more) drinks they were particularly proud of. We proceeded to have a great lunch, accompanied by three superb cocktails from their menu (hey, there were five of us!). One was the Calisco Punch (a delicious variation on the Pisco Punch, page 179), another was the Love Bizarre (a long drink made with muddled mint, shiso and fennel, mezcal, lime juice, cucumber juice, simple syrup, aloe liqueur, and bianco ver-mouth, and garnished with fennel, just bursting with flavor and bouquet), and the third was the Temptation Island.

Laura invented the latter as a "dealer's choice" for drinks writer Nissa Pierson, a friend and regular at Lo & Behold. "She has a blog called *My Herbal Roots* and she loves for us to make her cocktails that feature fresh herbs and bright flavors," Laura said. "It was an unusually hot night so I wanted to make an herbaceous Daiquiri-style cocktail but serve it over crushed ice to keep it extra-refreshing. To complement the green grassy flavors of the Kō Hana Agricole, I added the Four Pillars Olive Leaf Gin, which has myrtle, bay, and macadamia nut in the botanical mix. My business partner Tara Heffernon has a small farm where she grows herbs, edible flowers, and produce for the bar. Using fresh lemon verbena from our farm, and Cap Corse Blanc gave the drink floral aromatic and citrus notes. I opted for falernum as the sweetener for extra mouthfeel and tropical spice. It came out so nicely we put it on the menu!" I cannot agree more, and if you're in wine country, now you know where to go.

makes 1 cocktail

6 large lemon verbena leaves, plus several more for garnish

1½ ounces Kō Hana Hawaiian Agricole Rum

½ ounce Four Pillars Olive Leaf Gin (or another dry gin; see Note)

½ ounce Mattei Cap Corse Blanc

½ ounce John D. Taylor's Velvet Falernum

¾ ounce fresh lime juice

¼ ounce simple syrup (see page 6)

4 drops salt tincture (4:1 water to salt by weight)

Gently muddle the verbena leaves in a cocktail shaker to release their oils. Add the rum, gin, Cap Corse blanc, falernum, lime juice, simple syrup, and salt tincture to the shaker, along with some large ice cubes, and shake hard for 5 seconds. Strain into a metal julep cup filled with crushed ice. Garnish with lemon verbena leaves and serve with a straw.

---

note: If those with nut allergies have concerns about the gin having macadamia nuts in the botanical mix, the Four Pillars website (fourpillarsgin.com) has this statement: "Our Modern Australian Gin and Olive Leaf Gin both include macadamia nuts in the distillation process. Both gins have been tested and no nuts are detected in the final product, but we recommend checking with your doctor first!" Alternatively, Lo & Behold will make it with a different gin upon request—and you can too.

THREE DOTS AND A DASH

This is yet another tiki classic, invented during World War II by Donn "Don the Beachcomber" Beach. The name derives from the Morse Code rendering of the letter *V* as in "victory," which was used frequently during the war. It's also the name of one of the best tiki bars operating today, Three Dots and a Dash, which opened in 2013 in the River North neighborhood of Chicago. As with so many tiki classics, this drink has the simple Daiquiri as its core, with rum, fresh lime juice, and a sweetener (in this case a honey syrup). The recipe was lost for many years and was "discovered" by the intrepid tiki authority Jeff "Beachbum" Berry in time to be published in his 2007 book *Beachbum Berry's Sippin' Safari.*

makes 1 cocktail

1½ ounces amber Martinique rhum agricole

½ ounce Demerara rum

½ ounce fresh lime juice

½ ounce fresh orange juice

½ ounce honey syrup (see page 7)

Dash Angostura bitters

¼ ounce falernum

¼ ounce pimento liqueur (such as St. Elizabeth allspice dram)

6 ounces crushed ice

3 cocktail cherries, for garnish

Add all of the drink ingredients to a blender and blend at high speed for no more than 5 seconds. Transfer the contents into a stemmed goblet (a large wineglass will do), and garnish with the cocktail cherries on a skewer or cocktail pick.

TOM COLLINS
(AND HIS BROTHERS)

This drink, along with the Gin and Tonic, is one of the quintessential summertime refreshers. And it's so simple. As David Embury so succinctly noted in *The Fine Art of Mixing Drinks*, "the Collins is simply a Sour served in a tall glass with ice and charged water. Or, stated in another way, it is a lemonade made with charged water and spiked with gin or some other liquor." Over the past hundred-plus years, the name describes a simple mixture of London dry gin, lemon juice, sugar, and soda water, served on the rocks in its namesake Collins glass. Pretty simple, no? Well . . .

Over the years it's evolved, not so much in the components or ratios of the drink, but what people were calling it. Let's go back to London in the early nineteenth century, when an establishment called Limmer's Old House was in business, and its bartender/proprietor was one John Collins. According to cocktail historian David Wondrich, Collins was such a popular barkeep that he was the inspiration for a poem written by "two of the grandsons of the great playwright Richard Brinsley Sheridan," who also happened to be regulars at Limmer's. Part of the poem went like this:

> My name is John Collins, head-waiter at Limmers,
> The corner of Conduit street, Hanover Square;
> My chief occupation is filling of brimmers
> To solace young gentlemen, laden with care.

Yeah, they're just not writing 'em like they used to. Anyway, John Collins served a delightful punch made with genever, lemon juice, and sugar, and extended with soda water and ice. That drink was originally known as the John Collins. Easy to remember, John/genever. As the nineteenth century wore on, a sweeter style of gin gained popularity around the world, Old Tom Gin. So you had the John Collins being made with genever, the Tom with Old Tom. Okay, makes sense so far . . .

Then, at the turn of the last century, as London dry gin nudged Old Tom aside (*ageism* if I ever saw it), the Tom Collins became what we know today. But what about his brother John? As the twentieth century wore on, both genever and Old Tom gin continued to fall out of favor, and the name "John Collins" began to find itself attached to a Collins made with genever or whiskey. In two books from the late 1940s, *Bartender's Guide* by Victor "Trader Vic" Bergeron and Embury's, Bergeron called for bourbon while Embury stuck with a genever drink. (For what it's worth, Embury called the Bourbon Collins a "Colonel Collins," isn't that cute?) Toward the end of the twentieth century, the John Collins was a bourbon drink. And that's more or less the state of play in contemporary bars— however, it's anyone's guess whether you'll get genever, Old Tom, or something else in a Tom or John Collins in a craft cocktail bar today. Bartenders want to pay homage to this drink's rich history, and that's not a bad thing.

What follows is the "classic" Tom Collins recipe, followed by Embury's list of the recipes for Tom's brothers.

makes 1 cocktail

2 ounces London dry gin (Embury called for 3 to 4 ounces!)

1 ounce fresh lemon juice

½ ounce simple syrup (see page 6)

3 to 4 ounces soda water

1 lemon wheel, for garnish

Combine the gin, lemon juice, and simple syrup in a cocktail shaker filled with ice. Shake well and strain into a Collins glass filled with ice. Rinse the shaker (see page 5) with the soda water, then strain the soda into the glass. Garnish with the lemon wheel and serve with a straw.

recipe continues →

note: Although you can simply build this in the glass, I prefer to shake this drink to really extract the flavors from the lemon, get some good dilution, and chill the drink.

variations: To make a John Collins, use genever, or bourbon, as referenced above. The Mike (or Irish) Collins? Irish whiskey. The Jack (or Apple) Collins? Applejack. The Pedro (or Rum) Collins? Rum. The Pierre (or Brandy) Collins? Brandy or Cognac. The Sandy (or Scotch) Collins obviously has Scotch. And, of course, you've got your Rye, Canadian, Tequila, and Vodka Collins. To make a Hayes Fizz (invented by my friends Christy Pope and Chad Solomon at Milk & Honey in the 2000s), make a standard Tom Collins but rinse the glass (see page 5) with absinthe or Pernod first. To make a Grapefruit Collins, invented by bartending legend Vincenzo Errico, cut the lemon juice with grapefruit. Or try another Enzo creation, the Strawberry Collins, featuring gin, lemon and orange juices, simple syrup, one strawberry, and Schweppes lemon soda water. Or try Enzo's Bitter Collins (gin, Campari, grapefruit juice, lemon juice, simple syrup, and soda water), which is very similar to the creation of another Milk & Honey alum, Zachary Gelnaw-Rubin (he called his drink the Bicycle Thief). For a tiki take on the Collins platform, make it with pineapple juice, lemon juice, gold or amber rum, and soda water, garnished with a cocktail cherry and mint sprig, which renders the Tropical Collins, found in Jeff "Beachbum" Berry's 2007 book *Beachbum Berry's Sippin' Safari*. Lastly, I recommend to you my friend Danny Ronen's Cardamom Collins, which he makes like so.

CARDAMOM COLLINS

3 or 4 crushed cardamom pods, for garnish

1½ ounces No. 209 Gin (or any good American gin)

1½ ounces Don's Mix (see page 245)

½ ounce fresh lime juice

2 ounces club soda

1 grapefruit peel, for garnish

Crush the cardamom pods in a pint glass with a muddler or mortar and pestle, then set aside. Combine the gin, Don's Mix, and lime juice in a cocktail shaker filled with ice. Shake well and strain into a Collins glass filled with ice. Rinse the shaker (see page 5) with the club soda, then strain the club soda on top of the drink. Give the surface of the drink a good dusting of the crushed cardamom pods. Express the oils from the grapefruit peel over the top of the drink, then drop it in as a garnish.

THE GREAT TOM COLLINS HOAX OF 1874

Back before television brought us shows where wise guys were pranking innocent victims, American folk had to make their own such entertainment. For a perfect example of this phenomenon, submitted for your approval is "The Great Tom Collins Hoax of 1874."

Newspapers of the day carried breathless accounts of a pranking fad that was sweeping the nation. The hoax consisted of one saloon customer telling another, "Have you seen Tom Collins? He's been saying nasty things about you. He's down the street at such-and-such bar—go get him!" The poor, unwitting sucker would then proceed on a wild-goose chase from bar to bar. Newspapers joined in, publishing "Tom Collins sightings." It became rampant, until (presumably) everyone had caught on. At least one story ended tragically, with the enraged victim accidentally (and fatally) shooting himself during the fruitless search!

There were additional aspects to the pranking phenomenon. For example, theatrical performers, such as the Worrell Sisters and Harrigan & Hart, would advertise their variety shows by offering teasers that Tom Collins would make an appearance at their upcoming performance. Want to see Tom Collins? Go to Tony Pastor's Opera House in New York City, since "Tom Collins will be at the Matinee." An ad in the *New York Daily Herald* from May 3 stated, "I will be at Gleason's Billiard Room, 161 Bowery, every evening this week," and it was signed "Tom Collins." These sorts of shenanigans extended to such random things as fishing charter boats; if you went fishing on the ocean steamer *Seth Low*, for example, "Tom Collins, who has been going down to the banks over 21 years, will be on board."

The shameless hucksterism infiltrated Sunday church services, town hall meetings, and more. Pastors and ministers would advertise in the papers about an upcoming sermon; an ad in the *Brooklyn Daily Sun* of May 17, 1874, informed readers that Reverend Charles Everest would be preaching a sermon titled "Fools," and invited "inquirers after Tom Collins" to attend. The *Boston Globe* of May 25, 1874, advised readers to "Look out for Tom Collins at the Woman's Suffrage meeting, today."

Further, newspapers would create "fake news" items to join in on the fun. The *Georgia Weekly Telegraph, Journal and Messenger* of June 2, 1874, noted that "a great many persons in this city will, we know, be rejoiced to hear that notorious slanderer, Tom Collins, came very near being badly whipped last Friday night at Atlanta. He had been around at bar-rooms using foul language against various men not present. Two of the calumniated gentlemen armed with clubs got after him, and came within a half minute of catching him at Pease's restaurant." More than one newspaper announced that the "notorious humbug 'Tom Collins'" was hanged in effigy.

The legend of Tom Collins continued to have a moment in popular culture, with at least six popular songs being written in his honor. (In fact, sheet music for them is available on the Library of Congress website!) Eventually, like any fad, the Great Tom Collins Hoax faded, but there are still those who believe the John Collins became known as the Tom Collins simply because of the notoriety of the latter name.

TRINIDAD SOUR

When encountering this recipe for the first time, you might be tempted to think there's a typo. We're all used to seeing cocktail bitters being dispensed by the dash, not the ounce. Well, bartender Giuseppe González (see also the Painkiller, page 165) decided to go all in with this one, and it's an amazingly flavorful drink. But an ounce and a half of Angostura bitters in one drink?! Yes.

González created it in 2009, while working at Julie Reiner's Clover Club in Brooklyn. He was inspired by a cocktail that had come out the year before, the Trinidad Especial, invented by an Italian bartender named Valentino Bolognese. That drink won the Angostura European Cocktail Competition held in Paris in January 2008. The Especial contained one ounce of Angostura (even that amount was unheard of at the time!), among other ingredients. But, then again, perhaps Bolognese was himself inspired by the recipe for the Angostura Fizz (aka the Trinidad Fizz; see the Gin Fizz, page 102), found in Charles H. Baker Jr.'s 1939 *The Gentleman's Companion*, which also called for an ounce of Angostura, along with sugar, lemon or lime juice, egg white, and cream (ironically, Baker had the Angostura Fizz in a section of "Temperance Delights," as if they were nonalcoholic; Angostura clocks in around 89 proof!). The old saying about "standing on the shoulders of giants" must have been on González's mind as he decided to make his own riff on the Trinidad Especial. Despite its seemingly disproportionate proportions, it's become a modern classic.

1½ ounces Angostura bitters

½ ounce rye whiskey

1 ounce orgeat

¾ ounce fresh lemon juice

Combine all the ingredients in a cocktail shaker filled with ice. Shake well and strain into a chilled cocktail glass.

variations: As noted, see the Angostura Fizz, aka the Trinidad Fizz, with the recipe for the Gin Fizz (page OOO). Also try the Trinidad Especial (1 ounce of Angostura, ⅓ ounce pisco, 1 ounce orgeat, and ⅔ ounce fresh lime juice, shaken and strained).

WARD EIGHT

If each city has an (un)official or best-known cocktail, the Ward Eight would likely be Boston's. The most commonly told origin story concerns a local election back in 1898, when a candidate by the name of Martin Lomasney was running for an office in the state legislature. Lomasney represented Boston's Eighth Ward and was something of a political boss. He didn't have the nickname "Mahatma" for nothing. According to legend, Lomasney employed a somewhat cagey philosophy to ensure he always had plausible deniability in his various political maneuverings. His mantra? "Never write if you can speak; never speak if you can nod; never nod if you can wink."

As the story goes, members of the Hendricks Club, a social organization founded by Lomasney, were so certain as to the election's outcome that they held a victory party on election eve at the nearby Locke-Ober restaurant. That's right, on the *eve of the election!* No one was concerned they were tempting fate? Turns out they were right—Lomasney won. Further, a special drink was said to have been created for the evening, invented by bartender Tom Hussion. Or was it Billy Kane? Or was it Charlie Carter at the Puritan Club, five years later? In her contribution to *The Oxford Companion to Spirits and Cocktails*, Lauren Clark draws no conclusion. The recurring theme continues: success has many fathers.

What is certain is that the recipe shown below was found in a *Boston Herald* column in 1907. The drink enjoyed great popularity over the first half of the twentieth century. For example, in 1934 it was named as one of that year's top ten cocktails by *Esquire* magazine, which had only been launched the previous year. But, as was the case with so many classics, it fell out of favor and has only been revived in the past couple of decades.

2 ounces rye whiskey

⅝ ounce fresh lemon juice

1 teaspoon sugar

1 teaspoon grenadine

1 ounce soda water

1 orange slice, for garnish

Berries (your choice), for garnish

Combine the rye, lemon juice, sugar, and grenadine in a cocktail shaker filled with ice. Shake well and strain into a chilled cocktail glass. Rinse the shaker (see page 5) with the soda water, then strain the soda water into the glass. Garnish with the orange slice and whatever berries you choose.

WATERLOO

Looking for a delicious summertime refresher, and something to do with that watermelon left over from your last cookout? Here's your answer to both. This is one of my favorite drinks, and I especially love how the bitterness of the Campari works with the sour of the lemon and the sweet of the watermelon. The recipe is credited to Dushan Zaric and Jason Kosmas at Employees Only in New York City, circa 2012. That said, Jason tells me that "Dushan created it for a House of Campari event. It sold out in no time and we put it on the menu." Don't you love it when a bartender *doesn't* claim authorship of a great drink? It's become the king of Employees Only's line of tall drinks. The recipe is from Jason and Dushan's excellent 2010 book *Speakeasy: The Employees Only Guide to Classic Cocktails Reimagined.*

makes 1 cocktail

4 chunks of watermelon, about 1 by 2 inches each

¾ ounce simple syrup (see page 6)

1½ ounces Plymouth gin (or London dry gin)

½ ounce fresh lemon juice

½ ounce Campari

1 watermelon wedge, for garnish

Add the watermelon chunks and syrup to the shaker and muddle it well, until the fruit has turned into a juice. Then add the gin, lemon juice, and Campari, and add 5 large ice cubes and shake well. Transfer the mixture, unstrained (including the ice), to a tall Collins glass. Garnish with the watermelon wedge.

WATERMELON SOUR

Okay, two consecutive drinks featuring watermelon, and why not? This one comes from my dear friend Gina Chersevani. A New York transplant, Gina owns a classic dive bar in DC called Last Call, a block away from the flagship location of her local chain Buffalo & Bergen. (You need to visit next time you're in DC and get one her famous Lox'd & Loaded Bloody Marys; the garnish is a bagel with lox and cream cheese, so you get breakfast along with one of the best Bloodies you'll ever enjoy.)

As for the drink's creation, Gina explains: "I came up with this drink after doing a Food Network cooking show and 'sour' was the challenge given to competitors during one stage of the event. It dawned on me that things that start sweet, like melon, can sour in taste when they get overripe, which can create a really cool flavor. I paired that flavor with other sour components, like sour cream and vinegar, and I later carried that same idea into making this drink; This recipe is also excellent when making a nonalcoholic drink; just substitute Seedlip Garden 108 nonalcoholic spirit in place of the gin."

recipe continues →

4 or 5 watermelon chunks (ideally a bit overripe),
   or 1½ ounces watermelon water

1 teaspoon crème fraîche (or more, if you like)

Pinch of Maldon salt (or any coarse salt, just not iodized table salt)

1½ ounces vodka or gin (or a mix)

½ ounce fresh lemon juice

¼ ounce white balsamic vinegar

Soda water, to top

1 small watermelon wedge, for garnish

Combine the watermelon, crème fraîche, and salt in a cocktail shaker and muddle well, then add the vodka and/or gin, lemon juice, and balsamic vinegar. Fill the shaker about three-quarters full with ice, then shake well for about 15 seconds. Strain into an Old-Fashioned glass filled with ice and top with a splash of soda water. Garnish with the watermelon wedge.

WHISKEY SMASH

In *The Bartender's Guide*, Jerry Thomas succinctly defined the "Smash" as "simply a julep on a small plan." He offered three Smashes: the Brandy Smash, the Gin Smash, and the Whiskey Smash. Each one contained a half tablespoon each of sugar and water, and 2 ounces of spirit, along with 2 sprigs of mint, "pressed" or muddled well in the sugar and water. Each style of Smash was served in a glass two-thirds full of shaved ice, and garnished with another mint sprig. And that, ladies and gentlemen, was the Smash—for about 130 years! Then along came a bartender named Dale DeGroff, who tried something a little different and started a revolution in bartending.

After a legendary stint at the Rainbow Room, Dale remained in Manhattan to partner in the opening of a high-end bar and grill called Blackbird, circa 1999. He'd been familiar with Thomas's book since the mid-1980s, while he was working with restaurateur Joe Baum at Aurora, and decided that a new spin on a classic was in order. "I thought the julep could use some help," DeGroff told me, "especially Thomas's Smash version 'on a small plan.' Bourbon, sugar, and water didn't float my boat." So, he not only made one simple addition to the ingredients—lemon—but also took a quite literal approach to the category's name.

Starting with the classic "small plan" Mint Julep, he picked up his muddler and "smashed" some lemon wedges along with sugar and the mint. He added ice and the bourbon, and shook it well, then strained it over crushed ice. A star was born. He not only created a delicious new cocktail but launched a whole new category of drinks as well, which I've taken the liberty of calling the Twenty-First-Century Smash. Before long, bartenders all over the world would be smashing their own variations. Dale had smashed a path for others to follow. In the pages that follow, I'll talk about some other Twenty-First century Smashes, but first let's make Dale's Whiskey Smash.

recipe continues →

½ lemon, cut into quarters

2 or 3 fresh mint leaves

½ ounce simple syrup (see page 6)

2 ounces bourbon (Dale uses Maker's Mark)

1 mint sprig, for garnish

1 lemon wheel, for garnish

Muddle the lemon, mint leaves, and simple syrup in the bottom of a cocktail shaker. Add the bourbon and several ice cubes, and shake well. Strain into an Old-Fashioned glass filled with crushed ice. Garnish with the mint sprig and the lemon wheel.

variations: When in season, add some fresh peach slices to the ingredients to be muddled, and proceed as with the Whiskey Smash, and you've got Dale's Whiskey Peach Smash. Or use 2 ounces of Grand Marnier in place of the bourbon, and you've got a Grand Marnier Smash, invented by Zach Wilks, the lead bartender at Anthony's Chophouse, in the Indianapolis suburb of Carmel.

WHISKEY SOUR

Here's one of my favorite stories within Stanley Clisby Arthur's 1937 book *Famous New Orleans Drinks and How to Mix 'Em* (and believe me, for better or for worse, it's *full* of stories, and some of them are even true!). It concerns a Frenchman walking into a New Orleans cocktail lounge.

FRENCHMAN: Mix for me, *s'il vous plait*, a contradictions.
BARTENDER: A which?
FRENCHMAN: Zee great Américain drink—a contradictions.
BARTENDER: Never heard of it, mister . . . how's it made?
FRENCHMAN: You use whiskee to make eet strong; water to make eet weak; lemon juice to make eet sour, an' sugar to make eet sweet. Zen you say "here to *you*," an' you drink eet yourself! Zat, sar, ees zee contradictions.

Of course, the bartender knew what the Frenchman wanted, and *meexed heem* (sorry) "the old reliable, time-tested Whiskey Sour."

The Whiskey Sour is definitely "the old reliable, time-tested" drink Newspaper references to it date back to the 1860s: The *Rock Island Argus* of July 24, 1865, spoke of "a half dozen men want each a 'whisky sour' and go out rattling their big boots along the aisles and stairways, like so many horse's feet," and this whimsical poem appeared in the *Sioux City Journal* of June 12, 1877:

How doth the busy musquito [*sic*]
Improve each darkened hour;
And every time he bites a man.
Taste beer or whisky sour.

It's also one of the most popular drinks of all time (see Note). In the words of David Wondrich, in the revised edition of *Imbibe!*, "From roughly the 1860s to the 1960s, the Sour, and particularly its whiskey incarnation, was one of the cardinal points of American drinking." As the *Atlanta Daily Constitution* so deftly put it in 1879, "When American meets American then comes the Whisky Sour."

makes 1 cocktail

2 ounces whisk(e)y (your choice—bourbon, rye, etc.)

½ ounce simple syrup (see page 6), or ½ teaspoon sugar

½ to ¾ ounce fresh lime juice

1 ounce egg white (optional)

1 cocktail cherry, for garnish

1 orange slice, for garnish

If using the egg white, combine the whisk(e)y, simple syrup, lime juice, and egg white in a cocktail shaker without ice. Dry shake (see page 4), then add the ice and shake again for about 20 seconds. If omitting the egg, combine the whisk(e)y, simple syrup, and lime juice in a cocktail shaker filled with ice and shake well. Either way, strain into a chilled cocktail glass or an Old-Fashioned glass with a couple of large ice cubes in it. Garnish with the cherry and orange slice.

---

note: Now, you might wonder why you'll see the word spelled either "whisky" or "whiskey." There's no regulation or anything; however, the general rule of thumb is that American whiskeys, such as bourbon and rye, tend (I say *tend*) to spell it with the "e." The same is true with Irish whiskies. Scotch and Japanese, however, are spelled without the "e," as in "whisky." But that does not mean that Maker's Mark is Scotch (they forsake the "e" for some reason), or that an old recipe you might find for a drink made with "whisk(e)y" is one style or another. To add further confusion, one brand of Tennessee whisk(e)y spells it "whisky" (George Dickel), while another spells it "whiskey" (Jack Daniel's). It's enough to drive you to drink.

variations: There are so many! Add some cherry syrup to the drink and you've got an Armored Diesel (whiskey, lemon, simple syrup, cherry syrup), which was the "house drink" at the Officer's Club of World War II general George Patton's 2nd Armored Division. Or add a float (see page 5) of red wine and (maybe) a touch of orange juice and you've got a New York Sour or Claret Snap. Or replace half of the lemon juice with orange juice and you've made a Stone Sour (a pre-Prohibition favorite). (For what it's worth, in his 1917 book *The Ideal Bartender*, Tom Bullock made his Stone Sour with Old Tom Gin.) Also consider Jeffrey Morgenthaler's delicious Bourbon Renewal (bourbon, lemon juice, crème de cassis, simple syrup). Or try the Southern Sour (light rum, lemon, simple syrup, red wine as a float), or the Casanova Cobbler, invented by bartending great Erick Castro (rye, Punt e Mes, Cointreau, lemon juice, simple syrup). Then there's the Gold Rush (page 43), which calls for bourbon, lemon juice, and honey syrup. Another modern classic from Milk & Honey is the Kentucky Maid, invented by Sam Ross. It's a Whiskey Sour made with bourbon, lime juice, simple syrup, sliced cucumber, and mint leaves. Or consider this cheeky cocktail from the pages of Harry Craddock's *The Savoy Cocktail Book* (1930), the Rattlesnake Cocktail. It's nothing more than a rye Whiskey Sour, but with two egg whites and a dash of absinthe. Craddock noted that the drink was "so called because it will either cure a Rattlesnake bite, or kill Rattlesnakes, or make you see them." That Harry was quite the kidder. Then there's the Wildest Redhead, made with Scotch, lemon juice, honey syrup, and allspice dram, with a float of Cherry Heering, invented by Meaghan Dorman at Lantern's Keep in New York City. Another classic is the Monte Whiskey Sour, basically a Whiskey Sour with a little Montenegro Amaro added to it, along with egg white or aquafaba (see page 10). Lastly, try one of my all-time favorites, the Commodore (bourbon, lemon, and a dash each of crème de cacao and grenadine).

WHITE LADY

We're deep in the "W" section of this alphabetically organized book, and once again, I'm trotting out the line, "success has many fathers." While we know who *popularized* this drink, the jury is out on who *invented* it. It was, in fact, made famous by Harry Craddock, head bartender of the American Bar at London's Savoy Hotel and is found in his 1930 *The Savoy Cocktail Book* (the recipe shown here is from that book). This has led many to conclude that Craddock was the drink's creator. Then again, in Rosie Schaap's contribution to *The Oxford Companion to Spirits and Cocktails*, she points to a column written by one of the earliest (and most prolific) food and drink writers, G. Selmer Fougner, who wrote in the *New York Sun* that the drink originated at another London haunt, Quaglino's restaurant. A final, and perhaps more convincing, theory comes from my friend Simon Difford's excellent website, DiffordsGuide.com, where he points to a lovely 1934 advertisement for Booth's Dry Gin in the *Illustrated London News* showing bartender Victor Cabrin of London's Grosvenor House making a drink. It notes that Cabrin "has a remedy for 'blues' of every shade, his White Lady being perhaps his most famous."

Whoever its inventor was, the White Lady was a popular drink throughout the last century. According to Brian Van Flandern's book *Celebrity Cocktails*, it was one of Alfred Hitchcock's favorite drinks, and he'd have one any time he was at Harry's Bar in Venice, Italy. Another Harry's regular, Ernest Hemingway, had one of his characters ordering one at a bar in Bimini in *Islands in the Stream*. Unfortunately for the snooty-snoot customer, the bar was one of those "shot and a beer" joints, and the bartender was stumped (he referred to her and her ilk as "that trash comes in on yachts"). So he gave her a bottle of White Rock soda water. Folks, lesson learned: Just as you wouldn't ask for Lobster Thermidor at Cracker Barrel, don't order fancy cocktails at dive bars.

1½ ounces London dry gin

¾ ounce fresh lemon juice

¾ ounce Cointreau

Combine the gin, lemon juice, and Cointreau in a cocktail shaker with ice and shake well. Strain into a chilled cocktail glass.

---

note: Many recipes call for the addition of egg white, which you're free to use; Craddock's version goes without it.

---

variations: Use gin *and* applejack in equal amounts, lime juice, grenadine, and egg white, and make a Pink Lady. Or use white rum, orange liqueur, maraschino liqueur, lime juice, simple syrup, and egg white (or aquafaba; see page 10) for a Casablanca. Or use Old Tom Gin, both orange juice and lemon juice, and simple syrup, and you've made Tom Bullock's version of the Stone Sour as it appeared in his 1917 book, *The Ideal Bartender*. Or use London dry gin, pisco, bianco vermouth, and orange marmalade to make a Paddington Bear, invented by Simon Difford in 2014. For yet another great drink containing orange marmalade, see the similarly titled Paddington, described within the variations of the Daiquiri (page 75). If you want to further explore the idea of using a breakfast jam, try Sasha Petraske's Cosmonaut, which has gin, lemon juice, and raspberry preserves.

THE TWENTY-FIRST-CENTURY SMASH

This category would not be in this book were it not for my friend and mentor, legendary bartender Dale DeGroff. The Smash category of mixed drink dates to the nineteenth century, and it was, in the words of Jerry Thomas in his monumental *Bar-Tenders' Guide*, "simply a julep on a small plan." In other words, it consisted of spirit, sugar (or simple syrup, peach syrup, or other sweetener), ice, and mint. Thomas offered the Brandy Smash, Gin Smash, and Whiskey Smash. Again, Mint Juleps but slightly smaller.

But in the late 1990s, as the head bartender and co-owner of Blackbird in Manhattan, Dale decided to tweak the Smash. It's like he woke up one day and said, "I'm the king and I think I'll start a revolution in bartending. I'm going to take this category most people have never heard of, make *one tiny addition*, and create a whole new genre."

All he did was add a mere ½ ounce of freshly squeezed lemon juice to the drink. But he also prepared it a little differently from the original Smash, by muddling (or rather, *smashing*) the lemon wedges, simple syrup, and mint in a shaker. Then he added bourbon and ice, shook it well, and strained it into an Old-Fashioned glass filled with crushed ice. Lastly, he garnished it with a mint sprig and a lemon wheel. He called it the Whiskey Smash. It became a fixture at Blackbird, and Dale included it in his 2002 book *The Craft of the Cocktail*, which also featured what he called the Mandrin Smash (Absolut Mandrin vodka; half a lemon, quartered and muddled; and cherry brandy), the OP Smash, created by fellow Blackbird bartender and cocktail legend Audrey Saunders (OP brand Swedish flavored aquavit, lemon, simple syrup, and maraschino liqueur), and the Whiskey Peach Smash (whiskey, fresh peach, lemon juice, and simple syrup). Then, to even more firmly plant his flag on the beach, he put his now-famous Whiskey Smash on the bar menu at Bobby Flay's Bar Americain in 2005.

And thus, what I've come to call the Twenty-First-Century Smash was launched. Bartenders around the world took notice. Many were in New York City, but other amazing examples came from Boston, New Orleans, Indianapolis, and Hamburg, Germany. In the words of my friend H. Joseph Ehrmann, owner of Elixir Saloon in San Francisco, "We were smashing everything in a glass in SF!"

At Employees Only, bartenders Jason Kosmas, Dushan Zaric (see the Billionaire and Waterloo, pages 46 and 224, respectively), and the rest of the staff were inspired to create a whole suite of seasonal Ginger Smashes for their debut menu in the fall of 2004. One afternoon just prior to opening, they met at their "laboratory" in Williamsburg, Brooklyn, to test out their various recipes. As noted in their 2010 book *Speakeasy*, "The one cocktail that came out unexpectedly was the Ginger Smash. . . . Ginger has always been a favorite 'hot' ingredient of ours, but when we combined fresh cranberries and ginger root, muddled with sugar, the result was unlike anything we had tasted or made before." Try it, and I think you'll agree.

GINGER SMASH, WINTER SEASON

makes 1 cocktail

2 thin slices fresh ginger

10 fresh cranberries

1½ teaspoons superfine sugar

1½ ounces Plymouth gin

1½ ounces Berentzen Apfelkorn apple schnapps

¾ ounce fresh lemon juice

Muddle the ginger, cranberries, and sugar in a cocktail shaker. Add the gin, schnapps, lemon juice, and several ice cubes and shake well. Pour the contents of the shaker into an Old-Fashioned glass filled with ice.

Meanwhile, in another part of Manhattan, at Milk & Honey, Vincenzo "Enzo" Errico heard about the smashing (sorry) success DeGroff and others were having, and decided to create a Smash of his own, for a 2009 cocktail competition that was being hosted by Disaronno Originale (see the Amaretto Sour, page 34). Says Enzo, "So, I created this drink for the competition. I didn't win. But the drink is still very good, I believe." No arguments, here, Enzo.

SMOKY ALMOND SMASH

makes 1 cocktail

½ lemon, cut into 3 wedges

3 or 4 mint leaves, plus 1 mint sprig for garnish

1 ounce fresh grapefruit juice

¾ ounce simple syrup (see page 6)

1½ ounces Disaronno Originale

½ ounce Laphroaig 10-year-old single-malt Scotch

Muddle the lemon, mint leaves, grapefruit juice, and simple syrup in a cocktail shaker. Add the Disaronno, Scotch, and several ice cubes and shake well. Strain into an Old-Fashioned glass filled with crushed ice and garnish with the mint sprig.

In faraway Germany, inspired by DeGroff's innovation, bartender Joerg Meyer created his own Smash, but this time using another aromatic herb in place of the mint. This is a really delicious drink, and it continues to be a best seller at Le Lion in Hamburg.

BASIL GIN SMASH

makes 1 cocktail

1 ounce fresh lemon juice

¾ ounce simple syrup (see page 6)

2 basil sprigs

2⅓ ounces London dry gin (Joerg prefers Rutte)

Pour the lemon juice into a cocktail shaker, add the simple syrup and 1 basil sprig, and muddle. Add the gin and several ice cubes. Shake well and strain into an Old-Fashioned glass filled with crushed ice. Garnish with the remaining basil sprig.

---

note: Joerg also makes this with cachaça in place of the gin and calls it the Brazil Basil Smash. It's pretty delicious, as well!

Meanwhile, back in the States, bartender Anthony DeSerio decided to get in on the Smash game. He was helping to open a new bar in central Connecticut, in the summer of 2014, and he created a variation on the Mojito (page 154) using Plantation Stiggins' Fancy Pineapple Rum and called it the Smashing Punch. Later that year, Anthony went on a trip to Barbados and wanted the pineapple flavor in his drink to come from fresh pineapples, rather than an infused rum. Here's the result.

SMASHING PUNCH

makes 1 cocktail

¼ lemon, cut in half

3 or 4 large mint leaves, plus 1 mint sprig for garnish

2 ounces The Real McCoy 5 year single blended rum

¾ ounce Pineapple Syrup (recipe follows)

1 pineapple wedge, for garnish

Muddle the lemon in a cocktail shaker, expressing as much of its juice and oils as you can. Give the mint leaves a slap, add them to the shaker, and gently muddle them, taking care not to tear the leaves. Add the rum, pineapple syrup, and plenty of ice. Shake well, then strain into an Old-Fashioned glass over 1 very large ice cube. Garnish with the mint sprig and pineapple wedge.

PINEAPPLE SYRUP

makes 2 cups

1 cup Demerara sugar

1 cup fresh pineapple chunks

In a small saucepan, combine the sugar and 1 cup water and heat over low to medium heat until the sugar has dissolved. Add the pineapple, remove from the heat, and stir until the mixture cools to room temperature. Strain into a clean airtight container; discard the solids. Cover and store in the refrigerator. It will keep for about 3 weeks.

Another great Smash to come out of New York City comes from Nick Jarrett, who's now down in New Orleans at Holy Diver. But back in 2010, he was at Clover Club, in Brooklyn. Nick tells me:

> I was interested in lower-proof cocktails at that point, and I'd put a sherry-based Sour on the menu the previous rotation. So, I'd wanted to play further with the bitter/sour/sweet thing. Everyone was drinking Fernet-Branca like it was going out of style, and Carpano Antica Formula was the vermouth of choice. So, I figured smashing them together with a little salt and plenty of muddled lemon and mint might work. Prizefighter was just a punchy name—the original's full name was Prizefighter Smash No. 1. I did go on to make a whole series of variations with different amari and different styles of vermouth, some with overproof spirits to bring the drink up to standard proof. The joke was that the drink went to 11—you know, the classic *This Is Spinal Tap* reference.

PRIZEFIGHTER

makes 1 cocktail

3 or 4 lemon wedges

5 to 8 mint leaves, plus 1 mint sprig for garnish

¾ ounce simple syrup (see page 6)

1 ounce Fernet-Branca

1 ounce Carpano Antica Formula sweet vermouth

¼ ounce fresh lemon juice

Pinch of salt

Muddle the lemon, mint leaves, and simple syrup in a cocktail shaker. Add the fernet, vermouth, lemon juice, salt, and several ice cubes and shake well. Strain into an Old-Fashioned glass filled with cobble ice or crushed ice. Garnish with the mint sprig and serve with a straw.

Out in the Pacific Northwest at Artusi, the tiny Italian aperitivo bar adjacent to its sister restaurant, Spinasse, bartender Jason Stratton created a lovely new Smash using Averna, one of the most popular of Italy's bitter offerings. As background, Leo Leuci in *The Oxford Companion to Spirits and Cocktails* informs us that Averna was created in 1868 by Salvatore Averna, a textile merchant from Caltanissetta, Italy, at his country house in nearby Xiboli. What was different about Averna was the addition of Sicilian oranges and lemons to the conventional Italian amari formula, resulting in a product that was bitter but pleasant and somewhat sweet.

At Artusi, Stratton marries bourbon, Averna, walnut oil, muddled cherry and orange, and lemon soda to great effect. Here's how.

AVERNA SMASH

makes 1 cocktail

1 orange wheel

1 brandied cherry

½ teaspoon walnut oil (omit in case of a tree nut allergy)

2 ounces bourbon (Jason prefers Knob Creek)

1 ounce Averna

Fever-Tree bitter lemon soda, to top

Muddle the orange wheel, brandied cherry, and walnut oil in a cocktail shaker. Add the bourbon, Averna, and ice and shake until chilled. Strain into a Collins glass filled with ice and top with the lemon soda.

So, we've seen Smashes made with mint and basil, but how about arugula? Charlotte Voisey, portfolio ambassador at William Grant & Sons, thought arugula to be a splendid idea, wanting to draw upon the peppery notes found in that herb. She also wanted to use pineapple as her fruit, and had observed that oftentimes in cuisine, pepper can be used to draw out the flavors of fruits such as watermelon, strawberry, and pineapple. She chose to add to these peppery notes with her choice of spirit, Milagro Select Barrel Silver Tequila, which has a decidedly vegetal and peppery nose. The result is the Pineapple Arugula Smash, and it's delightful.

PINEAPPLE ARUGULA SMASH

makes 1 cocktail

6 fresh pineapple chunks (each about ¾ inch square)

½ ounce simple syrup (see page 6)

¾ ounce fresh lime juice

1½ ounces Milagro Select Barrel Reserve Tequila

2 small handfuls arugula leaves

Muddle the pineapple chunks and simple syrup in a cocktail shaker. Add the lime juice, tequila, half the arugula, and several ice cubes and shake well. Strain into an Old-Fashioned glass filled with ice. Garnish with the remaining arugula.

Lastly, bringing this global revolution back to New York, Frank Caiafa, formerly of Peacock Alley of the Waldorf-Astoria Hotel, created his tasty twist on the Smash and, in doing so, offers a delicious recipe for berry-infused gin.

BLUEBERRY AND BASIL SMASH

makes 1 cocktail

2 ounces Berry-Infused Gin (recipe follows)

1 ounce fresh lemon juice

½ ounce simple syrup (see page 6)

½ ounce egg white

5 basil leaves

Combine the gin, lemon juice, simple syrup, egg white, and 4 basil leaves in a cocktail shaker without ice. Dry shake (see page 4), then add ice and shake again for 10 seconds. Strain into an Old-Fashioned glass filled with ice and garnish with the remaining basil leaf.

BERRY-INFUSED GIN

makes one 750 mℓ bottle

1 (750 ml) bottle Farmer's Botanical Small Batch Organic Gin

1½ cups frozen blueberries

Pour the gin into an airtight glass container, then add the blueberries. Let stand at room temperature for 7 to 10 days. Strain the gin and discard the solids, then return it to the original bottle and seal. It will keep at room temperature for about 3 months.

WINTER SOUR

This is another really nice low(er)-ABV (alcohol by volume) drink. Bay Area bartender H. Joseph Ehrmann created this gem for a panel discussion at the Commonwealth Club in San Francisco in early 2009. Says he, "Each of us on the panel was asked to present a cocktail in an 'audience favorite' style competition, and this drink lost by one vote to my friend Jeff Hollinger. I think he rigged it." I suspect H. was being facetious. He also offers a nonalcoholic version, recipe below. I love to see cocktails with bitter aperitivo and citrus (see also the Jungle Bird, page 121; Select Aperitivo Sour; and the Waterloo, page 224). As to why H. suggests you muddle the rosemary separately, he says, "I always muddle before putting in the juice because the rosemary stays in the tin and doesn't stick to the muddler. If you muddle into the juice, you often end up with rosemary on the muddler, and then you have to knock the muddler against the tin a few times to free it."

makes 1 cocktail

2-inch-long rosemary sprig, plus another sprig for garnish

1½ ounces fresh Meyer lemon juice (see Note)

1 ounce egg white

1 ounce Campari (or use Stirrings blood orange bitters, pomegranate juice, or cranberry juice for a nonalcoholic version)

1½ ounces clover honey syrup (see page 7)

Strip the needles off the rosemary sprig, add them to your cocktail shaker, and muddle lightly. Add the lemon juice and egg white and dry shake (see page 4). Add the Campari and honey syrup, then add ice and shake well for 10 seconds. Strain into a chilled cocktail glass. Garnish with the second rosemary sprig.

---

note: If you don't have Meyer lemons, either use Eureka lemons, or mix ⅔ fresh lemon juice with ⅓ fresh orange juice.

ZOMBIE

The first full year for Americans to *not* have to worry about Prohibition was 1934. So you'd think that most bar owners would be content to offer pretty much anything to customers. The thinking might have been: As long as it was legal, had liquor in it, and tasted okay, the American consumer wasn't fussy (and wouldn't be for many decades). The bar (no pun intended) was pretty low. So why would one particular bar owner decide to create a whole concept around escaping to Polynesia to enjoy an exotic (and entirely phony—Pacific islanders certainly weren't drinking any of the concoctions being served in tiki bars!) island libation? That man was Ernest Raymond Beaumont Gantt, who, after legally changing his name to Donn Beach, opened the world's first tiki bar, Don's Beachcomber (which would later become Don the Beachcomber), in a Hollywood hotel lobby. From that humble beginning a cultural phenomenon was launched that, despite a two-decade hiatus beginning in the 1980s, is still thriving today.

According to tiki guru Jeff "Beachbum" Berry, in his contribution to *The Oxford Companion to Spirits and Cocktails*, "this powerful punch was the first famous 'tiki drink.'" Beach kept the recipe a secret, as was the case with most tiki drinks. For example, a staff bartender might make a drink with the mysteriously titled "Don's Mix" (recipe follows), not knowing that it was nothing more than white grapefruit juice and cinnamon syrup. (In case you're curious, Don's Mix No. 2 was a 1:1 blend of vanilla simple syrup and allspice dram.)

The Zombie developed a whole mystique about it, thanks in part to the fact that movie stars, columnists, comedians, and cartoonists ate, or rather *drank* it up. "Beware, in your Hollywood visit, never to have a Zombie . . . for you will never be the same," warned one article. Don also enforced a two-drink limit, adding to its mystique.

1½ ounces gold Puerto Rican rum

1½ ounces gold Jamaican rum

1 ounce 151-proof Lemon Hart Demerara rum (see Note)

¾ ounce fresh lime juice

½ ounce Don's Mix (2:1 ratio of white grapefruit juice and cinnamon syrup; see page 7)

1 teaspoon grenadine

6 drops Pernod (or other anise-flavored spirit, such as Herbsaint)

1 dash Angostura bitters

1 mint sprig, for garnish

Combine the rums, lime juice, Don's Mix, grenadine, Pernod, and bitters in a blender with ¾ cup crushed ice, then blend at high speed for no more than 5 seconds. Pour into a tall glass, add ice to fill, and garnish with the mint sprig.

> **note:** If you do not have or wish to purchase the rums listed above, don't despair—my old pals Jeff Berry and Ed Hamilton have you covered. They teamed up to make Hamilton Beachbum Berry Zombie Blend Rum, and it's sensational. Also, B.G. Reynolds offers a Paradise Blend (Don's Mix), should you not want to make your own.

FOR FURTHER READING

Alan, David. *Tipsy Texan: Spirits and Cocktails from the Lone Star State*. Kansas City, MO: Andrews McMeel Publishing, 2013.

Amis, Kingsley. *Everyday Drinking*. London: Bloomsbury Publishing, 2008.

Arnold, Dave. *Liquid Intelligence: The Art and Science of the Perfect Cocktail*. New York: W. W. Norton & Company, 2014.

Baker Jr., Charles H. *The Gentleman's Companion: Vol. II, Being an Exotic Drinking Book; Or, Around the World with Jigger, Beaker, and Flask*. New York: Derrydale Press, 1939.

Bergeron, Victor ["Trader Vic"]. *Bartender's Guide*. New York: Garden City, 1947.

Berry, Jeff ["Beachbum"]. *Beachbum Berry's Sippin' Safari: In Search of the Great "Lost" Tropical Drink Recipes and the People Behind Them*. New York: Cocktail Kingdom, 2007

———. *Beachbum Berry's Potions of the Caribbean: 500 Years of Tropical Drinks and the People Behind Them*. New York: Cocktail Kingdom, 2014.

Blocker, Jack S., David M. Fahey, and Ian R. Tyrrell, eds. *Alcohol and Temperance in Modern History: An International Encyclopedia*. London: Bloomsbury Publishing, 2003.

Brown, Derek. *Mindful Mixology: A Comprehensive Guide to No- and Low-Alcohol Cocktails with 60 Recipes*. New York: Rizzoli, 2022.

Cate, Martin, and Rebecca Cate. *Smuggler's Cove: Exotic Cocktails, Rum, and the Cult of Tiki*. Berkeley, CA: Ten Speed Press, 2016.

Clisby Arthur, Stanley. *Famous New Orleans Drinks and How to Mix 'Em*. New Orleans, LA: Harmanson, 1937.

Conolly, Charlie. *The World Famous Cotton Club: 1939 Book of Mixed Drinks*. American Spirits, 1939.

Craddock, Harry. *The Savoy Cocktail Book*. London: Constable & Co., 1930.

Crockett, Albert Stevens. *Old Waldorf Bar Days: With the Cognomina and Composition of Four Hundred and Ninety-One Appealing Appetizers and Salutary Potations Long Known, Admired and Served at the Famous Big Brass Rail; also, a Glossary for the Use of Antiquarians and Students of American Mores*. New York: Aventine Press, 1931.

DeGroff, Dale. *The Craft of the Cocktail: Everything You Need to Know to Be a Master Bartender, with 500 Recipes*. New York: Clarkson Potter, 2002.

———. *The New Craft of the Cocktail: Everything You Need to Know to Think Like a Master Mixologist, with 500 Recipes*. New York: Clarkson Potter, 2020.

Embury, David A. *The Fine Art of Mixing Drinks*. London: Faber and Faber, 1948.

Ensslin, Hugo R. *Recipes for Mixed Drinks*. 1916.

Escoffier, Auguste. *Le Guide Culinaire: Aide-Mémoire de Cuisine Pratique*. Paris, 1903.

EUVS Vintage Cocktail Books Collection, euvs-vintage-cocktail-books.cld.bz.

Felton, Eric. *How's Your Drink?: Cocktails, Culture, and the Art of Drinking Well*. Evanston, IL: Agate Surrey, 2007.

Gascoigne, George. *A Delicate Diet for Daintiemouthde Droonkardes; Wherein the Fowle Abuse of Common Carowsing, and Quaffing with Hartie Draughtes, Is Honestlie Admonished*. London, 1576.

Greene, Philip. *To Have and Have Another: A Hemingway Cocktail Companion*. Rev. ed. New York: TarcherPerigee, 2015.

———. *The Manhattan: The Story of the First Modern Cocktail*. New York: Union Square & Co., 2016.

Haigh, Ted ["Dr. Cocktail"]. *Vintage Spirits and Forgotten Cocktails: From the Alamagoozlum to the Zombie; 100 Rediscovered Recipes and the Stories Behind Them*. Beverly, MA: Quarry Books, 2004.

Jones, Stan. *Jones' Complete Barguide*. Los Angeles: Barguide Enterprises, 1977.

Kosmas, Jason, and Dushan Zaric. *Speakeasy: The Employees Only Guide to Classic Cocktails Reimagined*. Berkeley, CA: Ten Speed Press, 2010.

Lowe, Paul E. *Drinks: How to Mix and How to Serve*. Philadelphia: David McKay, 1909.

MacElhone, Harry, and Wynn Holcomb. *Barflies and Cocktails: 300 Recipes*. Paris: Lecram Press, 1927.

Meier, Frank. *The Artistry of Mixing Drinks*. France: Fryam Press, 1936.

Mustipher, Shannon. *Tiki: Modern Tropical Cocktails*. New York: Rizzoli, 2019.

Poister, John. *The New American Bartender's Guide*. New York: Signet, 1989.

Regan, Gary. *The Joy of Mixology, Revised and Updated Edition: The Consummate Guide to the Bartender's Craft*. New York: Clarkson Potter, 2018.

Schmidt, William. *Fancy Drinks and Popular Beverages: How to Prepare and Serve Them*. New York: Dick & Fitzgerald, 1896.

Simonson, Robert. *A Proper Drink: The Untold Story of How a Band of Bartenders Saved the Civilized Drinking World*. Berkeley, CA: Ten Speed Press, 2016.

Spary, E. C. *Eating the Enlightenment: Food and the Sciences in Paris, 1670–1760*. Chicago: University of Chicago Press, 2012.

Straub, Jacques. *Drinks*. Chicago: Hotel Monthly Press, 1916.

Tarling, William. *Café Royal Cocktail Book*. London: Sidney Press, 1937.

Thomas, Jerry. *The Bar-Tenders' Guide: A Complete Cyclopedia of Plain and Fancy Drinks*. New York: Dick & Fitzgerald, 1862.

Will-Weber, Mark. *Mint Juleps with Teddy Roosevelt: The Complete History of Presidential Drinking*. Washington, DC: Regnery History, 2014.

———. *Muskets & Applejack: Spirits, Soldiers, and the Civil War*. Washington, DC: Regnery History, 2017.

Williams, Ian. *Rum: A Social and Sociable History of the Real Spirit of 1776*. New York: Bold Type Books, 2006.

Wondrich, David. *Imbibe!: From Absinthe Cocktail to Whiskey Smash; A Salute in Stories and Drinks to "Professor" Jerry Thomas, Pioneer of the American Bar*. Rev. ed. New York: TarcherPerigee, 2015.

———. *Punch: The Desires (and Dangers) of the Flowing Bowl*. New York: TarcherPerigee, 2010.

Wondrich, David, and Noah Rothbaum, eds. *The Oxford Companion to Spirits and Cocktails*. Oxford University Press, 2021.

ACKNOWLEDGMENTS

Big thanks, as always, to my amazing literary agent and good friend, Adam Chromy of Movable Type Management, and to my tremendous editors, Caitlin Leffel and Elizabeth Smith of Union Square & Co.: It was a joy working with both of you! Thanks also to my publisher, Amanda Englander, for once again putting her faith in me. I also need to thank Jennifer Williams, formerly of Union Square, who originally extended the offer to me to write this book.

To the many friends, both in the cocktail world and also cocktail enthusiasts, who generously offered me their insights in response to my innumerable crowdsourcing posts on Facebook and Instagram, and other random inquiries, notably Rebecca Ahnert, Louis Anderman, Michael Anstendig, Christopher Bird, Laura Baddish, Kate Bouterie-Sporcic, Alexandra Bowler, Maxwell Britten, Derek Brown, Jared Brown, Shane Byous, Frank Caiafa, LaNell Camacho Santa Ana, Lizzy Caston, Merryll Cawn, Cheryl Charming, Lindsay Marsh Chatfield, Jennifer Colliau, Gary Crunkleton, Nick Crutchfield, Jason Crawley, Edward D'Antoni, Rachel Delston, Dimitre Darroca, Diana Danaila, Doy Demsick, Anthony DeSerio, Marco Dionysos, Megan Downes, Phil Duff, Josh Edwards, H. Joseph Ehrmann, Camper English, Jennifer English, Vincenzo Errico, Phoebe Isabelle Esmon, Travis Fourmont, Blair Frodelius, Kelly Gherkin, Richard Cannonball Gillam, JK Grence, Abby Gullo, Dave Hansen, Craig Hicks, Stefan Heubner, Ted Haigh, Khaled Hajj, Robert Hess, Brien Hoefling, Jason Horn, Craig Judkins, Gabrielle Kaufman Sterba, Scott Krinsky, Sam Kershaw, Lisa Laird Dunn, Ginny Landers Dowd, Chris Lang, Drew Larsen, Steven Robert LeBlanc, Matthew Lemle Amsterdam, Elizabeth Lloyd-Kimbrel, Nicholas Lowe, Todd "Mac" Macdonald, Steve Maroma, Seth Marquez, Sam Meyer, Anistatia Miller, Chris Milligan, Justin Michael Morales, Lauren Mote, Ingrid Neilsen, Craig Nelson, Ashley Newton, Bill Norris, Kate O'Neil, Effie Panagopoulos, Joe Pereira, Julie Pitts Talbert, Gabi Porter, Henri Preiss, Billiam Prestwood, Anand Rao, Drew Record, Julie Reiner, Joe Riley, Christopher Ritch, Brian Robinson, Danny Ronen, Piotr S-k, Audrey Saunders, Paul Sauter, Manuel

249

Schlüssler, Jack Sileo, Christopher Sinclair, Josh Snider, Eileen Spata, Joe Spata, Sean Spata, Raymond Stencel, Dave Stolte, Vern Stoltz, Kevin Stroud-Kroon, Chuck Taggart, Jo-Jo Valenzuela, Alex Velez, Brian Van Flandern, Artura Vera-Felicie, Jonathan Weston, Zachari Wilks, Mark Will-Weber, Angus Winchester, Damian Windsor, Xania V. Woodman, Michael Wyatt, and Karah Wylie.

To my great, great friends at Prestige Ledroit Distributing Company and Haus Alpenz, namely Michael Cherner, Jake Parrott, Eric Seed, and Chris Schmid, for donating their excellent products so I could fine-tune many of the recipes found herein.

Also to the fine folks at Fresh Victor, Liquid Alchemist, Ripe Bar Juice, Shaker & Spoon, Twisted Alchemy, and Yuzuco, notably Ingrid Achhorner, John Badalati, H. Joseph Ehrmann, Sonia Holstein, Maggie Lavengood, Griffin Owens, Danny Ronen, and Randy Tarlow, for sending me samples of their fine juices and syrups.

Lastly, to my beautiful and always patient wife, Elise, and our three fabulous daughters, Hannah, Madeleine, and Liv, for putting up with my occasional grouchiness, time spent away from the family, and all the unpleasantness that can accompany writing a silly little cocktail book. But hey, they also got to sample a few along the way, so there's that!

INDEX

**UNION
SQUARE
& CO.**

NEW YORK

ISBN 978-1-4549-4602-1
ISBN 978-1-4549-4603-8 (e-book)

For information about custom editions, special sales, and premium purchases, please contact specialsales@unionsquareandco.com.

Printed in China

2 4 6 8 10 9 7 5 3 1

unionsquareandco.com

Editor: Caitlin Leffel
Cover Design and Illustrations: Lisa Forde
Interior Designer: Stacy Forte
Project Editor: Ivy McFadden
Production Manager: Terence Campo